Champions

The 1998 New York Yankees

Champions

The 1998 New York Yankees

By the staff of The New York Times

ISBN 0-9668659-0-1
Manufactured in the United States of America
First printing 1998

CHAMPIONS: THE 1998 NEW YORK YANKEES
Managing Editor: NANCY LEE
Text Editor: MIKE HALE
Picture Editors: STEVE JESSELLI, SARAH KASS
Production Editor: JIM MONES
Designer: BARBARA CHILENSKAS OF BISHOP BOOKS

SPECIAL THANKS TO: Penny Abernathy, Neil Amdur, Tim Anderson, Laura Billingsley, Morin Bishop,
Tom Bodkin, Tom Burke, Michalene Busico, Tom Carley, Andrea Cautela, Barbara Chilenskas,
Beth Flynn, Dave Frank, Pam Gubitosi, John Hammond, Jeff Honea, Stuart Lavietes, Mike Levitas,
Bert Lightbourne, Barbara Mancuso, Alyse Myers, the Picture Desk and Photo Lab of the New York
Times, Lee Riffaterre, Stephanie Rice, Ken Richieri, Claire Spezio, Lisa Tarchak, Kirsten Wilson.

CHAMPIONS: THE 1998 NEW YORK YANKEES was prepared by
Bishop Books, Inc.
611 Broadway
New York, New York 10012

Cover photograph:
CHANG W. LEE

10   9   8   7   6   5   4   3   2

Contents

Where Babe and Lou Keep Hitting Them Out

There is nothing subtle about Yankee history. It sits there, as permanent and solid as the monuments behind center field, and in

BY GEORGE VECSEY

The 1927 Yankees, with Gehrig (back row, far left) and Ruth (back row, fifth from left), are the standard against which all subsequent teams have been measured.

case you missed the point, there are the retired numbers jumping out at you from the scorecard.

That's right. They even list the 15 great Yankees among the active players, as if to overwhelm you with numbers:

1 Martin, 3 Ruth, 4 Gehrig, 5 DiMaggio, 7 Mantle, 8 Berra, 8 Dickey, 9 Maris, 10 Rizzuto, 15 Munson, 16 Ford, 23 Mattingly, 32 Howard, 37 Stengel, 44 Jackson.

Sometimes a team comes into Yankee Stadium and seems to be fending off the ghosts of Yankees past, all that power, all that finesse, wafting around in the somber Bronx air.

It used to happen regularly to the Red Sox in the 40's and the White Sox in the 50's and the Tigers in the 60's and the Royals in the 70's. They'd get ahead around the seventh inning and think maybe they had a chance to slip past the Yankees, break the terrible spell, and then, boom, the Babe or Lou would bust one, in absentia.

This is fertile ground, the soil of Yankee Stadium, as if nourished by the brilliant perspiration of the sporting deities who played there. Occasionally there is a fallow spell, but then the next generation of superstars sprouts in lush profusion.

This Yankee team, the one that began winning in 1995 and continued to blossom toward record-setting numbers in 1998, is an anomaly—so international, so diverse, so contemporary. Yet it plays the same kind of baseball—booming home runs, crisp base-running, alert defense, stalwart pitching—that marked all the other Yankee generations.

The Babe would love this team. ("You guys get that big from eating steak and drinking beer?" he might ask of the Creatine generation.) The Old Perfesser would love this team. ("This O'Neill throws a helmet just like Mantle did.") Elston Howard would love this team. ("How do you say 'brushback' in Japanese and Spanish?")

With apologies to the playwright John Guare, all the men on the monuments and the retired numbers in the scorecards are linked to this Yankee team by no more than eight degrees of separation, eight decades of Yankee superiority from the 20's to the 90's.

Derek Jeter, the hip-hop shortstop with the presence that inspired a thousand banners (some of them overt proposals), wears uniform No. 2,

The elegant DiMaggio, perhaps the ultimate Yankee, hit 361 home runs while striking out only 369 times.

as of yet unretired. Every Yankee fan knows this is also the number of the dour shortstop of the pre-MTV age, Frank Crosetti, who played from 1932 through 1948, from the age of Ruth and Gehrig to the age of Henrich and Reynolds. Here is the narrowest degree of separation: Crosetti, who turned 88 on Oct. 4, 1998, would visit the Yankees when they played in Oakland. He was far more gregarious than when he was the crabby third-base coach and militant hoarder of the ball bag, earning 14 more Yankee World Series checks from 1949 through 1964.

Jeter and Crosetti would greet each other in the visitors' clubhouse. The spry old high priest of the fungo bat would mutter about "all the baloney going on today"—meaning he had been under orders to salvage all baseballs during practice. While, "Geez, today they throw them into the stands."

What Crosetti and Jeter shared was a strain of ruthlessness, a zeal to win, perfectly expressed in what Hank Bauer once growled at the rookie Tony Kubek on opening day of 1957: "Hey, kid, don't mess with my World Series money."

There is formidable history in the New York Yankees, a reservoir of resourcefulness and skill.

With Berra (left) and Mantle on the squad in the 50's, it seemed a foregone conclusion that the Yankees would be playing in October.

The franchise did take a while to develop this drive. The Yankees of the first two decades may have been burdened with an unseen hex for having spirited the original Oriole franchise out of Baltimore in 1903, to some obscure location uptown in New York City. When the dues were paid, however, the Yankees became the most consistent team in American sports history—a straight and powerful line from Bob Meusel to Paul O'Neill, from Herb Pennock to David Cone.

The team of the 20's is known for Lou Gehrig and Babe Ruth clubbing the league into submission with the home run, a weapon Ruth had, if not invented, then certainly elevated to a daily threat. The rest of that team was solid, as Yankee teams almost always are—with center fielders

Few performers in World Series history have been as reliable in the clutch as Jackson, who led New York to a pair of titles in the 70's.

like Whitey Witt and then Earle Combs.

The team of the 30's survived the decline of Ruth, right up to the tragic illness of Gehrig, diagnosed in 1939. Bill Dickey was such a great catcher that his No. 8 would eventually have been retired even if a brickmaker's son named Berra had not worn it later.

The 30's saw the arrival of perhaps the ultimate Yankee—the seemingly effortless, quietly brilliant Joseph Paul DiMaggio, who performed what the great Frank Robinson still insists is the most underrated feat in baseball. No, not the 56-game hitting streak. In his career, DiMaggio hit 361 home runs and struck out only 369 times. (In these bulked-up days, some ersatz sluggers seem to strike out 369 times a season.)

The 40's began with a little shortstop named Phil Rizzuto beguiling people with his bunting. By the end of the 40's, there was a catcher named Yogi Berra who, for the good of the team, would patrol left field in the World Series. He once defined the killer shadows of Yankee Stadium during autumnal daytime games: "It gets late early out there."

The Yankees turned some people off with their grim reaping of pennants, but Berra gave a human face to the wrecking ball. So did a wisecracking left-hander from the streets of Queens, Whitey Ford. So did the manager of the entire 50's, Casey Stengel.

In 1951, before a preseason exhibition at Brooklyn's Ebbets Field, Stengel walked a sullen young outfielder, Mickey Mantle, out to the complicated angles of the right-field wall and fence, to show him how to play the caroms. Mantle could not seem to comprehend that the old man with wrinkles had once patrolled that very same field.

"He thought I was born old," Stengel muttered.

Oh, well. Mantle hit a ton of home runs for the old man, who would win 10 pennants in his 12 years as manager.

The 60's began with a crotchety new right fielder, Roger Maris, contributing two Most Valuable Player seasons, hitting 61 homers to break Ruth's record, and getting mostly grief for it.

The last gasp of that generation came in 1964, when Elston Howard, himself a former m.v.p., squatted his 35-year-old body behind the plate in 146 games, the most he would ever catch in a season, holding together an aging franchise for one more pennant.

Howard was the first player of color with the Yankees, who were a scandalous 15th of 16 major league teams to break the barrier. No wonder so many people rooted for the Dodgers of Jackie Robinson, the Giants of Willie Mays, the Pirates of Roberto Clemente, the Cardinals of Bob Gibson.

There then came an ice age of failure that is all too often personified by one player who was good enough

to last a decade at second base. A nice man, he hates to hear his generation called The Horace Clarke Years.

Before the 70's were over, there would be the decade of Thurman Munson and Reggie Jackson, two opposites who stared at each other across the chasms of the clubhouse, but helped win World Series in 1977 and 1978. Munson died when he crashed his own plane in 1979; Jackson chose to be depicted in a Yankee uniform in the Hall of Fame rather than the uniform of the splendid Oakland teams of his youth.

That same generation, spanning the 70's and the 80's, was enlivened by Billy Martin, a brilliant manager but erratic human being who loved the uniform so much that it consumed him.

The 80's belonged to Don Mattingly, Donnie Baseball, whose era ended with one of the classic post-season series, a draining five-game loss to Seattle in 1995.

Thus began a new era in Yankee history. (Did we mention they are owned by a shy and retiring chap named George M. Steinbrenner 3d?) When seasoned Joe Torre replaced driven Buck Showalter as manager, the tabloids greeted him with headlines like "Clueless Joe." However, Torre became a wise and patient manager for this diverse band.

There was a Panamanian and a Jamaican-born player, an Australian and even a Japanese, with his own interpreter. There was a Cuban-American with long roots in Florida and a Cuban pitcher who literally had arrived on a boat. There was a studious Puerto Rican classical guitarist named Bernie Williams, the most graceful Yankee on and off the field since Joe D. himself. And there was the intense pitcher David Cone, who pitched through health crises, always available to chat with the press. Then there was the aforementioned Derek Jeter, part black, part white, whose best friend on the team was the Puerto Rican catcher, Jorge Posada. This was a team that even old Dodgers and Giants fans could like.

In a playoff game in the World Championship year of 1996, the Yankees were about to lose to the Orioles. Jeter, this man of the next century, hit a fly to right field that was ruled a home run when a kid reached out and touched the ball.

Yankee luck. Nothing new there. The kid did not mean to affect history—he just wanted a souvenir. My theory has always been that Billy Martin reached out and swatted it with desperate, spectral hands.

With all that history, all those numbers, on the Yankees' side, it is rarely an even battle.

Donnie Baseball owned the 80's, but never made it to the World Series.

The Regular Season

A Season To Savor

BY BUSTER OLNEY

Lounging in Joe Torre's office in spring training, George Steinbrenner was feeling good about how the Yankees looked. Steinbrenner asked aloud, Has any team finished 162-0? And Torre, cigar in hand, was not sure if the principal owner was joking.

The Yankees did not win 162 and lose 0 in 1998, but they came closer to doing so than any team since the advent of the 162-game schedule in 1961. They won a staggering 114 games, an American League record, and lost 48. They came within two victories of matching the single-season record of 116 victories, set by the 1906 Chicago Cubs.

They opened the season with three consecutive losses but finished with seven consecutive victories. In between, David Wells pitched a perfect game against the Minnesota Twins. The Cuban defector Orlando Hernández wept at the end of his long journey to the big leagues and then won 12 games. David Cone, his career sabotaged by an aneurysm and shoulder trouble the last two years, won 20 games for the first time since 1988. Darryl Strawberry revitalized his career, not knowing that the pain he began feeling in August was from a cancer. The Yankees brawled with Baltimore after the Orioles' Armando Benitez drilled Tino Martinez in the middle of his back, and when the Yankee Stadium field was cleared, Tim Raines hit a home run on the next pitch. It was the proper punctuation: You cannot beat us. The team's alliance and determination that night touched Torre.

The Yankees wrapped up a playoff spot sooner than any team ever had, and on that day, they did

A record 114 victories and a perfect game from Wells (opposite) were just two of the highlights in the Yankees' historic season.

From start to finish, New York was a *team*. Brosius beat Baltimore in July with a run-scoring single in the ninth and then was mobbed at the plate by his teammates, including Williams (in glasses) and Raines (31).

not realize they had clinched; Chad Curtis innocently flipped the game ball into the stands. When they stumbled in September, with only numbers to chase, Torre angrily challenged them to push themselves, and they responded.

The Yankees led the league in runs scored, allowed the fewest runs, ranked third in fielding percentage, second in stolen bases. Ten players, including the September comet Shane Spencer, hit 10 or more home runs, tying a major league record. The Yankees' record was 102–1 when leading after eight innings, a reflection of their bullpen.

Bernie Williams won the American League batting title, with a .339 average. Spencer hammered three grand slams in 10 days, as many grand slams as Torre had during his entire playing career. Scott Brosius drove in 98 runs, Derek Jeter accumulated 203 hits, Paul O'Neill batted .317 and drove in 116 runs, Martinez drove in 123 runs and slugged a team-high 28 home runs.

Joe Girardi, the everyday catcher in 1996 and 1997, ceded the No. 1 job to Jorge Posada without complaint. "It's not my place to say who should play," Girardi said, simply. Strawberry shared playing time with Raines and Curtis, and even when he was healthy and wanted to play more, he accepted his part-time role. Ramiro Mendoza was shifted to the bullpen when Hernández was promoted to the big leagues, admitted he wasn't happy but added that his first priority was to help the team win in any way. The regulars rested regularly and grumbled but understood, as Torre played his bench.

All year, the Yankees played down the significance of their success, saying it was something they would think about in the future. But as the playoffs began, some of them began acknowledging they were playing for their own corridor of history.

Success in the post-season, said Williams, "is very important."

"It's what we've been looking forward to since we got to spring training," he said. "We never knew how far we were going to get—we knew that if we played hard, we'd get into a position to be where we're at. Although it's been a very special year for me, and the team individually, we're still looking ahead. We still have some work we need to do, and we're looking forward to the challenge."

The sterling starting staff handled by Torre (above) was greatly buoyed by Hernández (left), whose heroic odyssey to the major leagues began with a perilous journey in a makeshift boat.

The falling expansion joint wreaked havoc on Loge Box A, Section 22 (above), forcing the Yankees to play Anaheim in Shea Stadium (top), the home of their crosstown rivals, the Mets. The Yankees, who had lost four of their first five games, would beat the Angels, 6–3, to extend their season-righting winning streak to six.

A Road Trip (to Queen:

April 15, 1998—The Yankees will play Anaheim in Shea Stadium at 12:05 P.M. today, and they will be the home team. If you have tickets for a game in the Bronx today, they will be honored in Queens.

Such is the confusion wrought by the 500-pound expansion joint that fell through the underside of the upper deck at Yankee Stadium on Monday, taking out Loge Box A, Section 22, Seat 7 hours before the Yankees were to play the Angels. The Stadium is closed until city inspectors say otherwise, and the Yankees, the most famous team in baseball, do not have a home for now. As of last night, they did not know where their next series would be played.

Like high school kids traveling to play cross-city rivals, the Yankees will dress in their home locker room at Yankee Stadium today. Then, in full uniform, they will board three buses and head across town to Shea Stadium, the first bus departing at 7 A.M.

"It's a huge distraction, there's no two ways about it," said David Cone, one of several Yankees who used to call Shea Stadium home. Mel Stottlemyre, the pitching coach, was once the Mets' pitching coach. Darryl Strawberry was the right fielder of the Mets' team that won the World Series in 1986. Manager Joe Torre managed the Mets from 1977–81. It will be better to be in the third-base dugout, Torre joked, because he did not have much success in the first-base dugout.

The Yankees, hampered by rain for the first week of the season and losers of their first three games, have won their last five. Now this. "There is a lot of speculation over what this is going to do to our team," Cone said. "None of it is good. Maybe in the long run this will bring us closer, but right now, those questions are kind of tough to answer."

As the Yankees stood for the anthem before their home opener (right), who could have predicted the historic season to come?

May

Just Perfect

MAY 17, 1998—Nervousness gnawed at David Wells in the seventh inning, when he began realizing that he might pitch a perfect game. He wanted the roaring Yankee Stadium crowd to remain silent, and he desperately needed his superstitious Yankee teammates to speak and ease the mounting tension.

But nobody would oblige him, save for David Cone, who removed his good-luck sunglasses and approached Wells. "I think it's time," Cone said, his delivery perfectly dry, "to break out the knuckleball."

Wells burst out laughing, and though he found himself shaking in the ninth inning, his fingers numb to the feel of his final pitch to Minnesota's Pat Meares, he completed the 15th perfect game in major league history, beating the Twins, 4-0. The only other perfect game at Yankee Stadium, and the only other one by a Yankee, came on Oct. 8, 1956, when Don Larsen beat the Brooklyn Dodgers in Game 5 of the World Series.

When Meares's soft fly ball dropped into the glove of right fielder Paul O'Neill, the burly and balding Wells bent down and thrust his left fist into the air, and then again. "This is great, Jorge, this is great," he yelled to catcher Jorge Posada, over and over.

After Wells hugged other Yankees and rode off the field on the shoulders of his tallest teammates, Darryl Strawberry and Bernie Williams, and after he emerged from the dugout to acknowledge one last and long salute from the crowd, a phone call awaited him. Don Larsen was on the line, and he confirmed to Wells that yes, the only two pitchers to throw perfect games in Yankee Stadium attended the same high school, Point Loma High of San Diego. Larsen, Class of '47; Wells, Class of '82.

"Right now, I'm the happiest man on earth," Wells said later, seeming genuinely humbled.

"He won't forget it," Larsen said. "He'll think about it every day of his life, just like I do."

The parade of zeros on the scoreboard (above, left) made it perfectly clear just what Wells had accomplished; after Meares flied out to end the game, Wells, all 245 pounds of him, was hoisted aloft by his jubilant teammates (above). The victory boosted the New York record to a gaudy 28–9.

STANDINGS · MAY 1

EASTERN DIVISION

Team	Won	Lost	Pct.	GB
New York	17	6	.739	—
Boston	18	8	.692	½
Baltimore	14	13	.519	5
Tampa Bay	12	14	.463	6½
Toronto	10	16	.385	8½

CENTRAL DIVISION

Team	Won	Lost	Pct.	GB
Cleveland	14	12	.538	—
Kansas City	12	15	.444	2½
Minnesota	11	16	.407	3½
Chicago	10	15	.400	3½
Detroit	6	18	.250	7

WESTERN DIVISION

Team	Won	Lost	Pct.	GB
Texas	18	8	.692	—
Anaheim	15	11	.577	3
Oakland	12	14	.462	6
Seattle	12	15	.444	6½

The acquisition of Chuck Knoblauch put Luis Sojo (left) on the bench for much of the year and helped create the depth that would carry the Yankees through the long season.

Taking Off the Gloves

MAY 19, 1998—The Yankees went from a perfect game Sunday to the most imperfect of games tonight.

After Bernie Williams slammed a three-run homer with two outs in the eighth against Armando Benitez, Baltimore's hulking, hard-throwing reliever, Benitez drilled Tino Martinez in the upper back with his very next pitch. The umpire, Drew Coble, ejected Benitez with a wave of his arm.

Benitez stepped toward home plate. Martinez glared at Benitez, and players slowly emerged from both dugouts. Darryl Strawberry came out pointing at Benitez, who dropped his glove and beckoned the enemy team. The Baltimore players met the Yankees, en masse, near the mound, some pushing, some shoving.

The Yankee relievers charged in from their bullpen, led by Graeme Lloyd, who ran at Benitez and began swinging, and a free-for-all ensued. Benitez retreated to the mouth of the Orioles' dugout, where other Yankees starting rushing him.

Jeff Nelson broke away and began swinging at Benitez, and finally Strawberry attacked, hitting Benitez in the face with one hard, overhand swing. Alan Mills, the Baltimore pitcher, jumped on Strawberry, and the fight exploded into the Orioles' dugout, hands grabbing, fists flying, nobody sure who was trying to stop the fight and who was trying to continue it.

It was frightening confusion; veterans said later it was among the nastiest fights they had witnessed. When players finally began to calm, Torre led Strawberry away and slowly, the Yankees returned to their dugout. Lloyd, Strawberry, Nelson and Mills were ejected.

Bobby Munoz replaced Benitez, and Tim Raines slammed a two-run homer. It was, Torre said later, the best way to respond, though Torre obviously was satisfied his players stood up for each other in the fight. "It was a reaction," he said, "that doesn't surprise me and doesn't displease me."

Scott Brosius (opposite), acquired from Oakland in a shrewd off-season deal, became a fixture at third base, hitting .300 and driving in 98 runs on the season.

After Martinez (below, hatless and restrained) got plunked by Benitez, all hell—and both benches—broke loose; the Yankees would go on to win the game by 9–5.

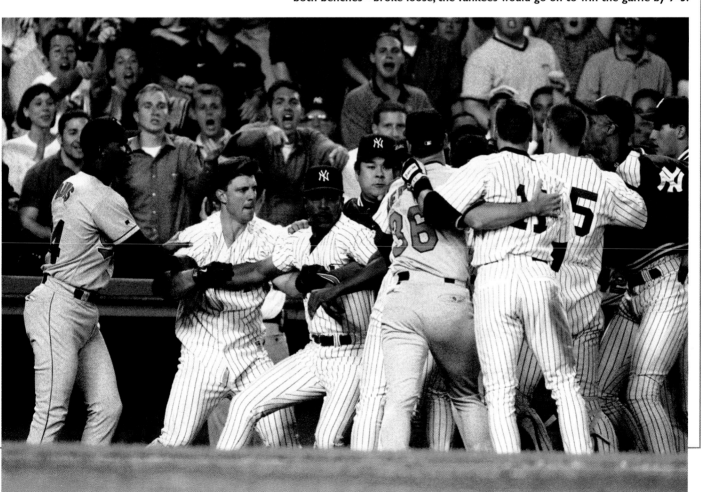

June

El Duque was sky-high (above) even before his first major league start; by the time Torre congratulated him (left) after the Yankees' 7–1 victory, the Cuban defector, less than six months away from his treacherous journey to freedom, was living his American dream.

Safe at Home

JUNE 3, 1998—Before throwing his first pitch tonight, Orlando Hernández stood behind the mound for several seconds and stared around at Yankee Stadium. These were moments to remember, the realization of a lifelong goal and the culmination of a harrowing journey that began six months ago with a risky escape from Cuba and ended on baseball's grandest stage.

Forbidden to play baseball in Cuba by officials who feared that he would defect, Hernández, known as El Duque, survived that trip in a makeshift boat and signed with the Yankees. He performed so well in the minor leagues that he was promoted to pitch at Yankee Stadium tonight. The crowd roared when he was introduced, cheered him when he walked to the mound and burst out with more cheers when he struck out the game's first hitter, Quinton McCracken. He left the game after seven innings, getting the victory as the Yankees defeated Tampa Bay, 7–1.

On the morning of Dec. 26, Hernández and seven others, including his wife, Noris Bosch, got on a 20-foot sailboat made of scraps, carrying only several cans of Spam, some fresh water and sugar. It was a dangerous flight. After 10 hours, they landed on Anguilla Cay, a deserted spit of land; for several days they huddled under a sail for warmth and survived on seaweed and conch. They were spotted by a United States Coast Guard helicopter and transported to the Bahamas.

At a recent Columbus Clippers game, a large contingent of Cuban-Americans waved flags and banged drums. An hour after the game, in the parking lot, the drumbeats could still be heard outside the stadium—a group of 20 or so playing music. In the middle of them, Orlando Hernández danced.

And last night at Yankee Stadium, he completed his long journey and pitched.

STANDINGS · JUNE 1

EASTERN DIVISION

Team	Won	Lost	Pct.	GB
New York	37	13	.740	—
Boston	31	22	.585	7½
Toronto	28	27	.509	11½
Baltimore	25	30	.455	14½
Tampa Bay	24	30	.444	15

CENTRAL DIVISION

Team	Won	Lost	Pct.	GB
Cleveland	32	22	.593	—
Minnesota	24	29	.453	7½
Chicago	22	31	.415	9½
Detroit	21	30	.412	9½
Kansas City	21	32	.396	10½

WESTERN DIVISION

Team	Won	Lost	Pct.	GB
Texas	33	21	.611	—
Anaheim	27	26	.509	5½
Seattle	26	29	.473	7½
Oakland	22	31	.415	10½

David Cone, with a little help from his friends, won 11 games by the end of June to lead the Yankee staff.

New York—New York

JUNE 26, 1998—Rivers of blue caps formed in the aisles at Shea Stadium after the eighth inning. They were Mets fans, defeated, depressed and departing. Above them, a mocking chorus started: "Na, na, hey, hey, goodbye." The Yankee faithful serenaded their counterparts as they headed for the trains and the parkways and the bridges.

The Yankees own the city's bragging rights for at least one day after beating the Mets, 8–4. They trailed, 4-3, before Paul O'Neill smashed a three-run homer in the seventh inning off Mel Rojas, discouraging most of the 53,404 who made up the largest crowd of the year at Shea. Derek Jeter, the Yankees' shortstop, guessed that 65 percent to 70 percent of the fans were rooting for the Mets, "because I got booed pretty good."

O'Neill stood in the on-deck circle watching Rojas warm up in the seventh, and remembered: good fastball, great forkball. Look for something to hit hard. Don't get behind. "I faced him in the National League," O'Neill said later, "and had no success whatsoever."

Rojas fired his first pitch, a forkball. A hanging forkball. O'Neill reached across the plate and swung, the ball rocketing toward left-center field.

At Yankee Stadium, the fence in left-center field bows outward, a Death Valley for fly balls like this one. But in Shea Stadium, left-center field is a cozy 371 feet away, and with a light breeze blowing in that direction, the ball kept going. "I'm glad we played here," O'Neill said.

In the third inning, some fans had begun chanting for the Yankees, but the Mets fans drowned them out. Darryl Strawberry, a veteran who has witnessed many memorable games at Shea, sat next to the rookie Homer Bush.

"Homer," Strawberry said, "this is baseball. This is as good as it gets."

Hideki Irabu, the Yankee acquisition from Japan who was 6–3 entering the series against the Mets, got rocked, surrendering 4 runs in 5⅔ innings, before Ramiro Mendoza and then Mariano Rivera entered the game and shut the Mets down.

Paul O'Neill (below) was the star of Game 1 in the Mets-Yankees series, going two for five with a home run and three r.b.i.; Derek Jeter (opposite, fielding ball) drove in two runs in the Yankees' 7–2 victory in Game 2.

EASTERN DIVISION

Team	Won	Lost	Pct.	GB
New York	.56	20	.737	—
Boston	.48	32	.600	10
Toronto	.42	41	.506	17½
Baltimore	.37	46	.446	22½
Tampa Bay	.34	47	.420	24½

CENTRAL DIVISION

Team	Won	Lost	Pct.	GB
Cleveland	.46	34	.575	—
Minnesota	.38	43	.469	8½
Kansas City	.36	45	.444	10½
Chicago	.33	48	.407	13½
Detroit	.31	48	.392	14½

WESTERN DIVISION

Team	Won	Lost	Pct.	GB
Anaheim	.49	32	.605	—
Texas	.46	36	.561	3½
Oakland	.37	44	.457	12
Seattle	.34	49	.410	16

Runaway

JULY 5, 1998—The last time a major league baseball team won 61 of its first 81 games, Theodore Roosevelt was President of the United States, Franklin and Eleanor Roosevelt were newlyweds and a precocious child named George Herman Ruth, later known as the Babe, had just left his father's saloon in Baltimore for a school for wayward boys. The last time until today, that is, when the Yankees defeated the Baltimore Orioles to make their record 61–20, equaling the marks of the 1907 Chicago Cubs and the 1902 Pittsburgh Pirates.

The Yankees of 1927 are generally considered to be the greatest team in baseball history, their lineup graced by the famed Murderers' Row; that group won 57 of its first 81 games. Whether the Yankees of 1998 will be compared favorably to the 1927 Yankees, the 1961 Yankees, the 1976 Cincinnati Reds or any of baseball's other great teams will depend on whether they continue to win at such an astounding rate, and whether they win the World Series.

The lineup is stocked with stars, like Paul O'Neill, but also with capable veteran role players, like Darryl Strawberry, and a pitching staff that includes the likes of David Cone and David Wells.

Beyond the talent, however, the Yankees seem to possess a karma; good things happen for them. Orlando Hernández, the defector from Cuba who has been a wild success, was promoted to the big leagues last month only because a Jack Russell terrier bit Cone on the hand. Today, the Yankees scored the only run of their game against Baltimore when Chad Curtis was hit by a pitch with the bases loaded.

"They have their own little 'Truman Show,' " said Scott Erickson, the losing pitcher, referring to the movie about a man who doesn't know his life is scripted to perfection. "Everything goes right for the Yankees."

With manager Joe Torre (opposite, above) pulling all the right strings, the Yankees (above) gelled into a magnificent sum of some very talented parts; they won their first five games in July to surge to 61–20 and send their fans into a frenzy of celebration (opposite, below).

Routine Thrills

OAKLAND, CALIF., AUG. 4, 1998—The Yankees chewed on the post-game spread tonight minutes after the second game of their doubleheader sweep. Seated at tables in the visitors' clubhouse, they watched the highlights.

There was Darryl Strawberry, hammering the game-tying, pinch-hit, ninth-inning grand slam they will remember at Old-Timers' Days decades from now.

The Yankees scored nine runs in the ninth inning of Game 2 and turned a 5–1 deficit into a 10–5 victory, their 80th. Two-thirds of the way into the season, what seemed absurd now seems possible: the Yankees are on a pace to win 120 games, which would shatter the American League and major league records. They've made the unimaginable routine.

Oakland's Kenny Rogers, who left in the ninth inning holding that 5–1 lead, said, "They are by far the best team I will ever face."

With the bases loaded and nobody out, Strawberry walked to the plate, pinch-hitting for Joe Girardi. The ungraceful arrogance of Strawberry's days with the Mets has been stripped away. He is 36 years old, limping on a knee he believes is arthritic. But this has never changed: He loves to play baseball, he knows he can hit a baseball, and he seemed quite certain he was going to hit the baseball a long way when he stepped in against Bill Taylor. He was correct.

Rounding first base and seeing the ball disappear over the center-field wall, Strawberry, a self-trained stoic now, could no longer mute his emotion, and he grinned. He had hit a ninth-inning grand slam, like so many ballplayers have imagined.

Ejected from his seat by the sound of Strawberry's bat redirecting Taylor's pitch, Derek Jeter began screaming: "He got it! It's gone!" The instinct, players said, was to run to home plate and high-five Strawberry and hug him. The raw emotion, Girardi mused later, almost felt like high school.

"That's the kind of excitement this team feels day in and day out," he said. "And we're pretty lucky."

An August miscellany: Orlando Hernández produced an array of K's (above) after striking out 13 Texas Rangers in a 2–0 Yankee victory; Bernie Williams (opposite, below) was once again vying for the league batting title, hitting .352 as of Aug. 14; Scott Brosius (opposite, above) threw out Mark McLemore in the Yankees' 6–5 victory over Texas, New York's 10th in 11 games.

STANDINGS · AUGUST 1

EASTERN DIVISION

Team	Won	Lost	Pct.	GB
New York	.76	27	.738	—
Boston	.63	44	.589	15
Baltimore	.55	54	.505	24
Toronto	.54	56	.491	25½
Tampa Bay	.43	63	.406	34½

CENTRAL DIVISION

Team	Won	Lost	Pct.	GB
Cleveland	.62	46	.569	—
Minnesota	.51	56	.477	10½
Kansas City	.48	60	.444	14
Chicago	.47	60	.439	14½
Detroit	.44	63	.411	17½

WESTERN DIVISION

Team	Won	Lost	Pct.	GB
Anaheim	.58	50	.537	—
Texas	.57	51	.528	1
Oakland	.48	60	.444	10
Seattle	.48	60	.444	10

Take Pictures. Fu

Yankee stopper Mariano Rivera
(right) had good reason to
smile in August as New York
began to watch the rest of the
American League recede in
its rearview mirror.

The Stealth Clinching

A couple of near misses: Tino Martinez (above, right) missed home plate and was eventually tagged out by Kansas City catcher Mike Sweeney; but no matter, the Yanks won the game anyway, 8–2; Chad Curtis (above) caught, then dropped, this fly ball off the bat of Seattle's Russ Davis in a rare Yankee loss, 13–3 to the Mariners. It hardly mattered either, since the Yankees had quietly clinched a playoff spot the previous night.

AUGUST 29, 1998—The Yankees are so good that when they clinched a spot in the playoffs today—the earliest clinching date in the 20th century—they didn't even know it.

There were no group hugs, no popping of champagne corks. Nobody had a clue. The Yankees crushed Seattle, 11–6, scoring all their runs in the first four innings, and a sellout crowd filed out of Yankee Stadium, heartened by the team's fourth consecutive victory.

The Yankees enjoyed their post-game meal, watched Toms River, N.J., in the Little League World Series, showered and dressed. Players recounted the show put on by Derek Jeter, his three hits and four runs and his 17th home run. Nothing was said about the playoffs. They all went home.

More than an hour after the game, however, as stadium workers swept and cleaned the otherwise empty park, reporters re-examined the mathematics of the standings. At about 6:08 P.M., almost an hour and a half after David Segui's fly ball settled into Chad Curtis's glove for the final out, it was determined that the Yankees had clinched a playoff spot.

Nobody cheered. Nobody knew.

The Yankees have no one but themselves to blame for the confusion; they have won so often that qualifying for a playoff spot became inevitable. They posted a 61–20 record by the All-Star Game, and Manager Joe Torre has been answering questions about his playoff rotation for the better part of a month. The Yankees have maintained all along that winning 11 games in the post-season, and thus the World Series, is their ultimate goal, their entire focus. They proved this unwittingly yesterday.

Nobody drank champagne, nobody poured beer on a teammate's head, no television reporter was forced to sacrifice a suit. Nobody knew.

August

September

Shane Spencer's September was the stuff of dreams. After eight seasons in the minors, he was called up by the Yankees on Aug. 31 and proceeded to hit 10 home runs in 67 at-bats, including three grand slams in 10 days, one of them (above) in an 8–3 victory over Tampa Bay on Sept. 27.

The End of the Beginning

September 27, 1998—Videotaped memories of the 1996 World Series filled the TV screen in the players' lounge at Yankee Stadium this morning: Jim Leyritz hitting the pivotal home run, the large dark eyes of Joe Torre glazed with tears after the final out. Two years later the Yankees will pursue another World Series title. The goal is the same, but the stakes are higher: they will play for a place in history. They thumped Tampa Bay today, 8–3, and finished with 114 victories and 48 defeats. Only one other team won more regular-season games, the 1906 Chicago Cubs, who were 116-36.

But the Cubs lost the World Series. Should the Yankees win the Series, following one of the greatest regular-season performances, they could be called baseball's best team. Ever.

"Now we've got to get ready for the war," said George Steinbrenner, the team's principal owner. "We've just been in a battle up to now. I think there's a quality about this team. They're warriors."

The Yankees led the league in runs and allowed the fewest runs. They won the American League East by 22 games, the largest margin in club history.

They played hard. They always did.

Jay Tessmer is 26, a longtime minor leaguer who made his major league debut on Aug. 27. He remembers Mike Stanton welcoming him to the bullpen; he remembers how, when he was credited with the victory that night, all of the veterans congratulated him warmly, as if he had been around all season.

A small part of this club's legacy belongs to Tessmer. He knows he will probably not pitch in the post-season, and he packed a bag today, saving space for his Yankees jersey, No. 62. "I want my jersey," he said, laughing a bit. "I don't know if I have to pay for it, but I'm taking it."

He has thought about handing a picture of the 1998 Yankees to a grandchild and pointing to that serious-looking young man in the second row, between David Cone and Luis Sojo. That was me, he might say. That is me.

Tessmer, Williams, Cone. They all could live forever in their own corridor of history. The stakes are high.

For sheer excellence, Bernie Williams (top) may have been the Yankees' best; on the season's final day he went 2 for 2 to win the A.L. batting title (with a .339 average) and help New York to its 114th victory. Is it any wonder the Yankee faithful (above) felt grateful?

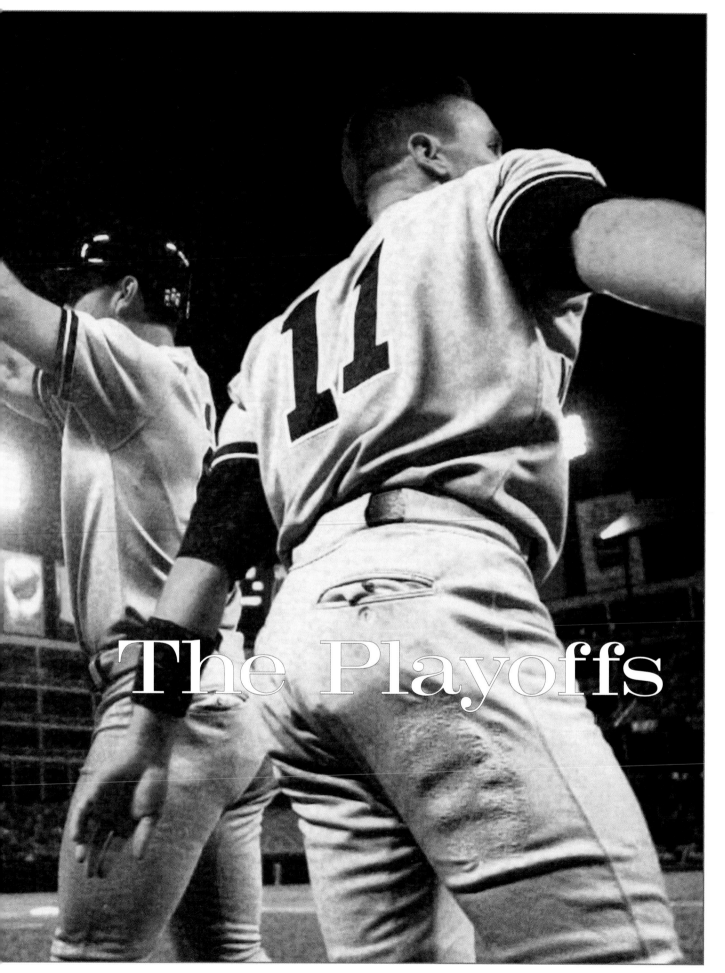

The Playoffs

No Time to Relax

The Yankees (left) basked in the applause from their fans (opposite) at the end of the regular season, but they were well aware that memories would mean little if the team faltered in the playoffs.

BY BUSTER OLNEY

What Joe Torre does better than perhaps any manager in baseball is take pressure off his players, relax them. He intended to work toward this end before the American League playoffs, to hold a meeting and tell the Yankees to keep doing what they had done all year and not worry about anything else.

But the reality of the Yankees' situation, Torre acknowledged later, would not permit this. All the players knew that if they lost in the playoffs, all that they had accomplished during the regular season would be remembered merely as the set-up for a cruel punch line. The 114 victories created such extraordinary expectations that anything other than total success in the post-season would be viewed as total failure.

None of the Yankees would be able to relax during the first two rounds, particularly the three-of-five-game division series with Texas, in which a couple of bad days could immediately smear their season—and the Rangers were a frightening team, with the slugger Juan Gonzalez and tough hitters like Rusty Greer, Will Clark and Ivan Rodriguez.

"Russian roulette," Torre called the five-game format. Said David Cone: "If we don't get to the World Series and finish it off, some of the luster will be taken off our record-breaking season. We want to finish it off."

O'Neill's seething intensity (opposite) served not only to motivate him but also to fire up his teammates (above).

Some of the Yankees were accustomed to playing tensely. First baseman Tino Martinez tortures himself after making outs, and many of Oakland's club officials felt Scott Brosius batted .203 for the A's in 1997 in large part because he was beating himself up over his slow start and lack of production.

But in tense times, Cone once suggested, the Yankees look to Paul O'Neill. No player performs under greater self-scrutiny than O'Neill, the All-Star right fielder renowned for his explosions after making outs. Jose Cardenal, the first base coach, hears O'Neill's self-indictments and tries not to laugh; he turns away if he can't help himself, his body shaking.

"Sometimes he's saying, 'I can't hit anymore, I'll never get another hit,' and he's batting .320," said Cardenal. "If he goes 0 for 3, that's the first thing he'll say: 'I can't play no more.' The guy just wants a base hit every time he bats."

If he makes the final out of an inning, O'Neill might slam his helmet after crossing first base. If O'Neill makes an out in the middle of an inning, he returns to the dugout with his head down, sometimes talking to himself. The bat boys who sit in the well near the Yankees' bat rack bend away instinctively, unsure of how O'Neill's momentary self-loathing might manifest itself.

"What happens with him is that frustration builds up," said Bernie Williams. "He might fail in his first at-bat, and then his second at-bat, and then in his third at-bat, if he doesn't have a hit, he's ready to explode. There's no telling what he's going to do if he goes 0 for 4."

The seething intensity apparently runs in the family. According to Irish tradition, two rival chieftains—including the leader of the O'Neill clan—agreed to row to the Isle of Destiny, and whoever touched it first would possess land rights. As they neared the island, the O'Neill leader realized he was going to lose. He drew his sword, cut off his left hand and threw it to shore, winning the race. The bloody hand—The Red Hand of Ulster—is part of the O'Neill coat of arms.

None of the Yankees actually carried a sword onto the field as the American League playoffs began, but one had the feeling they were ready to do what they had to, to validate their regular season and assure their place in history.

Game 1

Wells may have been running on fumes late in the game, but he still had enough gas to dispose of the Rangers in Game 1.

rotation, a decision that still bothers Wells. Coming off a season in which he went 18–4 and pitched a perfect game, however, Wells got the Game 1 assignment this year and justified that decision. With the top two buttons of his jersey undone and sporting a hint of a goatee, Wells challenged the Rangers all game.

The Yankees led by 2–0 in the seventh inning when Texas put together a couple of hits. With runners on first and second and two out, Wells jumped ahead of Mike Simms, no balls and two strikes, the Yankee Stadium crowd of 57,362 roaring. Simms fouled off a pitch, took two balls, then fouled off two more pitches with good swings. Wells had not allowed a three-run homer this year, and this did not seem like the best of times for the first one.

So Wells zipped a fastball inside, Simms staring at it, the crowd exploding. Ball 3. Wells turned away disgustedly as fans screamed at the plate umpire,

NEW YORK—Joe Torre jogged to the mound in the eighth inning tonight and invaded the personal space of David Wells, going chest to chest. Wells stepped back uncomfortably, but Torre moved forward, looking his pitcher directly in the eyes, and asked, "How are you feeling?"

This was no time for heroics. This was Game 1 of the American League division series, the Yankees leading Texas by two runs and Wells's pitch count nearing 130. How was he feeling? He was exhausted.

But Wells persuaded Torre to let him pitch out of trouble—and did so. Mariano Rivera closed out the Rangers in the ninth inning, preserving the 2-0 shutout.

"David was running on fumes out there at the end," Torre said.

Said Wells, "I strive for this kind of challenge."

A year ago, Torre placed Wells at the back of the Yankees' playoff

Jim Joyce. Jorge Posada signaled for a changeup, and Simms swung and missed. End of inning.

Wells returned to the mound for the eighth, fatigue setting in, his arm lagging. Mark McLemore doubled with one out, prompting Torre's visit.

"How are you feeling?" Torre asked. O.K., Wells replied.

"No—how are you feeling?" Torre asked, wanting to be convinced.

Posada stepped forward and said, "Joe, he's got it."

Torre nodded and ran back to the dugout. Wells struck out Roberto Kelly. Rusty Greer bounced a broken-bat grounder toward shortstop, Derek Jeter racing in and throwing to first for the third out. Wells pumped a fist.

For the Yankees, a team seeking its place in history, 1 victory down, 10 to go.

SEPTEMBER 29, 1998 ∗ YANKEES 2 ∗ RANGERS 0

Game 2

The scintillating Spencer continued to produce for the Yankees, ripping a solo home run (above) in the second inning—his eighth homer in 28 at-bats—and then singling and scoring on Brosius's two-run shot in the fourth.

NEW YORK—About 100 letters addressing Andy Pettitte's slump have landed in the locker of Mel Stottlemyre, the Yankees' pitching coach. Stottlemyre reads them all and dismisses them all, believing Pettitte has always possessed his own antidote.

A chronic self-doubter who slumped in the last two months of the regular season, Pettitte finally ignored the pressure he inflicts on himself. He concentrated solely on the glove of his catcher tonight and pitched seven strong innings as the Yankees defeated the Texas Rangers, 3–1, in Game 2 of the division series at Yankee Stadium.

"He's got a belly full of guts," Manager Joe Torre said.

The rookie Shane Spencer, a late insertion into the Yankees' lineup as the No. 7 hitter, hammered a home run and Scott Brosius, batting eighth, slammed a two-run shot, spurring the crowd of 57,360. The bottom third of the Yankee lineup has batted .529 in accounting for all five runs in the first two games.

It wasn't until the season's final week that Pettitte emerged from his funk—at about the same time Torre told Pettitte he would be part of the team's post-season rotation, which seemed to give the left-hander peace of mind.

"It feels great," Pettitte said last night, "because obviously there were a lot of people questioning Joe for starting me in Game 2."

Even as Pettitte warmed up for last night's game, Stottlemyre felt Pettitte was much different, much more confident, in deep concentration. Once on the mound, Pettitte seemed to be communicating only with Girardi's glove; see the glove, hit the glove.

"His focus," Stottlemyre said, "was as good as it can get."

Spencer smashed a thigh-high fastball over the left-center field wall in the second inning, beyond the 399-foot sign. It was

his eighth home run in 28 at-bats, dating to the last days of the regular season. He returned to the dugout grinning broadly, but the crowd would not let him sit until he acknowledged the cheers once more. On his next at-bat, with one out in the fourth, Spencer skipped a hard grounder through the middle. Brosius then launched a two-run shot beyond the fence in right field.

Pettitte retired the Rangers in order in the seventh, and his night was over. He had allowed three hits and one run in seven innings, no walks, eight strikeouts. Pettitte smiled widely afterward. This is what he needed.

SEPTEMBER 30, 1998 * YANKEES 3 * RANGERS 1

Game 3

The numeral on Cone's cap (above) was a poignant salute to Strawberry; O'Neill's solo shot (above, right) began the New York scoring.

ARLINGTON, Tex.—David Cone's quivering lower jaw stiffened earlier this week when someone asked him whether he would be able to pitch Game 3 after learning of Darryl Strawberry's cancer. "I'm going to be ready to pitch, I'll tell you that," Cone said, his voice instantly hardened.

Cone did not need another reason to compete, but he had one, and he was the winning pitcher as the Yankees beat Texas by 4–0 and completed, in bizarre fashion, a three-game sweep of the Rangers in the division series early this morning.

A Texas-sized storm descended on The Ballpark at Arlington and delayed the game for 3 hours 16 minutes. Play resumed at 1:24 A.M. New York time, and the final out wasn't recorded until 2:26.

The rookie Shane Spencer added to his growing legend by hitting a game-clinching three-run homer in the sixth inning—his second home run of the series and his ninth in his last 33 at-bats.

Spencer's home run seemed to come right out of "The Natural." As the sixth inning started with the game scoreless, the flags on the top rim of the stadium turned and stiffened, under attack from a northeast wind.

OCTOBER 2, 1998 * YANKEES 4 * RANGERS 0

Paul O'Neill waited on a curveball from Aaron Sele, the Rangers' starter, and smashed it over the wall in left-center field, scattering the Yankees' bullpen and giving New York a 1–0 lead. The wind began blowing harder.

Tino Martinez chopped a single and Tim Raines reached out and slapped a line drive toward the left-field corner. When Rusty Greer cut off the ball and kept it from bouncing against the wall, Martinez was forced to stop at third base. Dick Bosman, the Texas pitching coach, went to the mound to speak with Sele. During their conversation, rain began falling, and many fans rushed to find cover.

In Spencer's first at-bat, Sele had thrown him a curveball, and Spencer had taken a great swing but lifted a high fly to center field. Spencer grimaced in frustration after returning to the dugout, feeling he had missed a chance.

He probably walked to the plate thinking about that pitch. Sele spun another breaking ball. Spencer waited for it to curve downward, then dropped the head of his bat on the ball, blasting it to left field. Greer turned around and watched it disappear into the first rows of the stands for a three-run homer. Spencer circled the bases with a small grin on his face as the storm descended.

The three-run blast from Spencer (above, taking a champagne shower) put the Yankees in front by four runs, and Mariano Rivera settled matters by pitching a shutout ninth before being mobbed by his jubilant teammates (top).

Starting Strong

Game 1

LINE SCORE											
Cleveland	0 0 0	0 0 0	0 0 2	—2
New York	5 0 0	0 0 1	1 0 X	—7

NEW YORK—Scoring lots of runs early would be nice, Joe Torre mused before tonight's playoff game with Cleveland, as if he were considering a room service menu. And the Yankees delivered.

They pummeled the Indians' best pitcher, Jaret Wright, for five runs in the first inning and went on to win, 7–2, in Game 1 of the American League Championship Series. A crowd of 57,138 on a brisk fall evening at Yankee Stadium basked in the glow of this seemingly unbeatable team, a team that needs three more victories to reach the World Series for the second time in three seasons and the 35th time in franchise history.

Following a regular season in which they won 114 games, the most in A.L. history, the Yankees are doing everything right in the post-season. They swept Texas in the division series, limiting the heavy-hitting Rangers to one run in three games, and last night they rocked the Indians with an immediate burst of offense, consistently superb defense and more great pitching from David Wells, who shut out the Indians until allowing a two-run home run to Manny Ramirez in the ninth inning.

Otherwise, the Indians managed only four singles; the Yankees have allowed just 3 runs in 36 innings in the post-season. They have now won 118 games in the regular season and playoffs combined, matching a feat achieved by only one other team in baseball history: the 1906 Chicago Cubs, in a 154-game season and a six-game World Series.

Remarkably, the Yankees' confidence appears to be growing. "It's like a steamroller building up steam," said Chuck Knoblauch, their leadoff hitter.

The confidence, Torre suggested, is built on the 114 regular-season victories, the belief that if they approach the game the same way and play hard, they will win. Wells arrived at the Stadium this afternoon seeming self-assured and loose, wearing dark sunglasses, high-top basketball sneakers, blue jeans and a T-shirt. Fans waiting outside the players' entrance screamed for him, and Wells nodded: No problem.

Before the game, he playfully donned a black jersey, with the name of the heavy-metal band Metallica stripped across the front, and slipped into the dugout, jokingly suggesting that he might wear this particular uniform on the field. If Wells felt nervous in any way, he masked his feelings expertly.

Or maybe he and the Yankees have come to believe they are going to win every game. Wright must have felt that way right off the bat. He started for Cleveland, having beaten the Yankees twice in the playoffs last year; this year, he was one of only five pitchers who beat the Yankees twice in a regular season in which they lost only 48 of 162 games. But the Yankees dismissed him last night as if they were swatting away an annoying insect.

Wright likes throwing his fastball high in the strike zone, and the Yankees wanted to make him bring the ball down. Tim Raines had said that the Yankees wanted to get runners on base and make

O'Neill's single in the first inning (opposite) drove in Knoblauch with the Yankees' first run.

OCTOBER 6, 1998 * YANKEES 7 * INDIANS 2

Wright throw from the stretch position, rather than from a windup. "We just don't think he's as comfortable with runners on base," Raines said.

They tested this theory immediately. Leading off the bottom of the first, Knoblauch lined a single over second base, and Wright had to work from the stretch. Derek Jeter singled, with Knoblauch stopping at second.

Paul O'Neill battled Wright to a full count—Wright would throw 36 pitches in the first inning—and then, with both runners moving, O'Neill golfed a single to right, driving in one run. When Bernie Williams lined a single through the middle, Jeter raced home.

Four batters into their lineup, the Yankees had a 2–0 lead and two runners on base. Chad Ogea scrambled to start warming up in the Cleveland bullpen.

After a force-play grounder to second by Tino Martinez left runners at first and third, Martinez stole second as Raines struck out. There were two outs, and with another out, Wright would be in good condition.

But with Shane Spencer batting, Wright threw a curveball when it appeared that catcher Sandy Alomar was expecting a fast-ball, and the ball bounced between Alomar's legs for a wild pitch. O'Neill crossed the plate with the Yankees' third run. Spencer walked.

Everything was going wrong for Wright.

Jorge Posada lined a single, driving in another run, and Wright was finished. Because Wright broke Luis Sojo's left hand with a tight pitch in a spring training game, the Yankees have little regard for the Cleveland pitcher, and fans at the Stadium showed their disdain last night. As Wright walked off the field, head down, the crowd roared mockingly, thanking him for his effort.

"They got me," Wright said later. "Tomorrow is another day."

But the first inning was still not over. Scott Brosius singled off the reliever Ogea, driving in another run, and Wright's line was complete—two-thirds of an inning, five hits, five runs, one walk, one strikeout.

Wells had a big lead and used it to his advantage. Usually aggressive anyway, Wells challenged the Indians with fastballs, some sinking and some riding high in the strike zone.

Omar Vizquel got Cleveland's second hit of the game in the third inning, and Wells then struck out both Kenny Lofton and Joey Cora, two batters who have hit him hard in the past. He breezed, aided by a great play by Jeter at shortstop and Spencer's nice running catch in left in the sixth. Wells, Posada said, "was just able to relax."

All the Yankees appear relaxed, absolutely sure they are going to win. They have acknowledged the inherent pressure in playing the post-season after their stunning performance in the regular season. But there is inordinate stress on the Cleveland Indians, as well: after winning 89 games, 25 fewer than the Yankees, during the regular season and after seeing the Yankees' pitching completely dominate the Rangers in the first round, what is going through the minds of the Indians today?

David Cone will find out soon enough.

Jeter's rare blend of muscle and grace was on display when he went airborne to nail Travis Fryman.

Human

Game 2

LINE SCORE				
Cleveland	0 0 0	1 0 0	0 0 0	0 0 3—4
New York	0 0 0	0 0 0	1 0 0	0 0 0—1

NEW YORK—Bill Buckner is doomed to infamy for letting a grounder go through his legs in the 1986 World Series. Because of a mental blunder in the Yankees' playoff game tonight, Chuck Knoblauch is destined for a similar fate if the Yankees go on to lose the championship series to Cleveland.

Knoblauch stubbornly argued with an umpire as a Cleveland runner circled the bases with the tie-breaking run in the 12th inning—and as teammates and fans among the crowd of 57,128 at Yankee Stadium screamed for him to retrieve the baseball lying nearby. The Indians went on to win, 4–1, tying the series at one game apiece.

Knoblauch's mistake will be remembered by every baseball fan, serious or casual, and Little Leaguers will recite what coaches have been telling players since baseball began: Finish the play, then argue with the umpire.

"It was a helpless feeling watching the ball sit there and nobody going after it," said Jeff Nelson, the Yankees' losing relief pitcher.

So ended the Yankees' 11-game winning streak, which dated seven games into the regular season. So ended the notion that the Yankees would crush the Indians before storming into the World Series. The Yankees suddenly find themselves in a serious fight, with the next three games at Jacobs

OCTOBER 7, 1998 ∗ INDIANS 4 ∗ YANKEES 1

After All

Field, the frustration from tonight's game hanging over them.

Long before Knoblauch's mistake, the Yankees had had many chances to win. David Cone pitched valiantly, giving up five hits and one run in his eight innings. But the Yankees managed just seven hits, off seven Indians pitchers, in 12 innings and went 1 for 12 with runners in scoring position. They had a runner at second and nobody out in the ninth and couldn't score.

But nobody remembers Bob Stanley's pitching mistakes before Buckner's error in 1986; they remember the ball going through Buckner's legs, allowing the Mets to beat Boston in Game 6 and go on to win the Series in seven. This time, people will remember Knoblauch standing at first base, pointing for the umpire to make a call in his favor, as the ball rolled behind him.

Jim Thome opened the Indians' 12th with a single off Nelson, then was replaced by pinch-runner Enrique Wilson. Travis Fryman came to bat for the Indians, and everybody knew he would try to bunt.

Fryman bunted well, pushing the ball about halfway up the first-base line. From first base, Martinez charged in, the play more difficult than he expected. Fryman scampered toward first, running on the infield grass the whole way, inside the foul line. As Wilson raced toward second, Knoblauch moved to first to cover the base.

With no time for hesitation, Martinez whirled and fired toward first. Knoblauch started to reach for the baseball; wary of the oncoming Fryman, Knoblauch pulled away. The ball struck Fryman in the middle of the back an instant before his foot hit the base.

The ball bounced away, rolling to a stop on the infield dirt behind first base, as Knoblauch stood, arm outstretched, motioning for the home-plate umpire, Ted Hendry, to make an interference call.

Knoblauch's knucklehead play: Fryman (opposite) laid down the bunt; Knoblauch pulled away as the throw hit Fryman in the back (above, left); ignoring ball, runners and the screaming of the crowd, Knoblauch (above, right) argued with the umpires.

A game of inches: Paul O'Neill (opposite) made a brilliant diving catch, then held on to rob Joey Cora of a hit in the third inning; Shane Spencer (above) was unable to come up with Omar Vizquel's shot into the leftfield corner that went for a triple in the eighth.

Knoblauch came to a stop, but the world around him kept moving. Wilson rounded second. Rounding first, Fryman saw the ball on the ground, saw Knoblauch arguing and kept running. "I figured I would keep running until somebody told me to stop," he said.

As Knoblauch stood, pointing, Nelson and Martinez began yelling for him to get the ball. Teammates in the dugout were yelling. Wilson kept running, rounding third. Fans screamed at Knoblauch. Knoblauch pointed.

Finally, Knoblauch moved, charging back for the ball, throwing homeward, but off balance. Wilson stumbled, then dived across the plate with a headfirst slide. Safe.

Fryman was on third, and Joe Torre was sprinting from the Yankee dugout to argue. "It was a terrible call," a disgusted Torre said later as part of a rambling discourse on the play.

Later, Jim Evans, the umpires' crew chief, said that it didn't matter that Fryman was running on the grass, or that the ball hit him when he was in fair territory. The base is in fair territory, Evans said, and Fryman must be in fair territory when he touches it.

"The fact that he was literally on the base or right at the base when it hit him," Evans said, "he has a right to be in that position."

Evans saw a replay after the game. "I thought the call could've gone either way." he said. "I thought it was the right call in that situation."

George Steinbrenner disagreed. "Too bad this great game had to be decided by a call like that," he said.

The Indians added two more runs, on a single by Kenny

Lofton. Nobody will ever know whether they would have scored the runs anyway, even if Knoblauch had hustled to retrieve the ball or if the umpire had ruled interference, sending Wilson back to first with one out.

What the fans saw was Knoblauch standing and pointing as the tie-breaking run circled the bases, and when Knoblauch batted in the bottom of the 12th, he was booed lustily.

Afterward, Knoblauch did not really address why he didn't pursue the ball, at one point saying he should have looked for the ball and at another saying he wouldn't have done anything differently.

"It was so loud and so crazy, I didn't have any idea where the ball was," Knoblauch said. "After a little bit, I looked around and saw it back there."

Torre acknowledged that, blown call or not, Knoblauch should have pursued the baseball. "I watched the replay before I came in here, and he was yelling at the umpire and you can't do that," Torre said. "You have to make the play, and then go back and argue with the umpire. But I think he was just shocked that they didn't make the call."

Steinbrenner said: "He should've chased the ball. A guy under fire—I understand."

For now. Should the Yankees lose this series and the place in history they are pursuing after winning 114 games in the regular season, neither Steinbrenner nor history will be sympathetic to Knoblauch.

Just ask Bill Buckner.

A Night to Forget

LINE SCORE											
New York	1	0	0	0	0	0	0	0	0	—	1
Cleveland	0	2	0	0	4	0	0	0	X	—	6

CLEVELAND—The Yankees offered odes to confidence after their season of staggering achievement fell into jeopardy tonight. David Cone, Joe Girardi and others insisted that everything would be O.K., that the Yankees would ultimately prevail against Cleveland.

But their faces did not match their words; they sounded relaxed, but they looked tight and angry and concerned after Cleveland whipped Andy Pettitte, 6–1, to take a lead of two games to one in the championship series. Bartolo Colon started slowly for Cleveland, but finished with a four-hit victory that was backed by four home runs—three in a four-batter sequence in the fifth inning, including Jim Thome's second of the game.

George Steinbrenner watched sullenly, his chin tucked in his palm, looking like a kid staring outside on a rainy day. The Yankees won 114 games, swept Texas in the division series, scored five runs in the first inning of this championship series with Cleveland—and they are in trouble.

They are not hitting. Since collecting six hits and five runs in the first inning of Game 1, the Yankees have batted .167 in the last 29 innings and have scored just four runs. They have 3 hits in their last 24 at-bats with runners in scoring position.

"It's gut-check time," Cone said. "It's a real character test for this team. We need to come out and win tomorrow night and get the ball back to Boomer"—David Wells—"in Game 5. And we feel good about that."

On the heels of the Game 2 debacle, when Chuck Knoblauch argued with an umpire as the tie-breaking run circled the bases in the 12th inning, the Yankees needed a strong outing from Pettitte. But he was awful.

"It was just disappointing," Pettitte said, "because I really wanted to pitch a big game."

He fell behind in the count to 7 of the first 10 batters he faced, and when he risked throwing pitches over the plate, the Indians took full, destructive swings. Cleveland had runners at first and second with two out in the first inning, and Travis Fryman slammed a line drive to left—directly at Shane Spencer for the third out.

During the Yankees' endless fifth inning a grim Torre (above) removed Pettitte (opposite) from the game.

OCTOBER 9, 1998 * INDIANS 6 * YANKEES 1

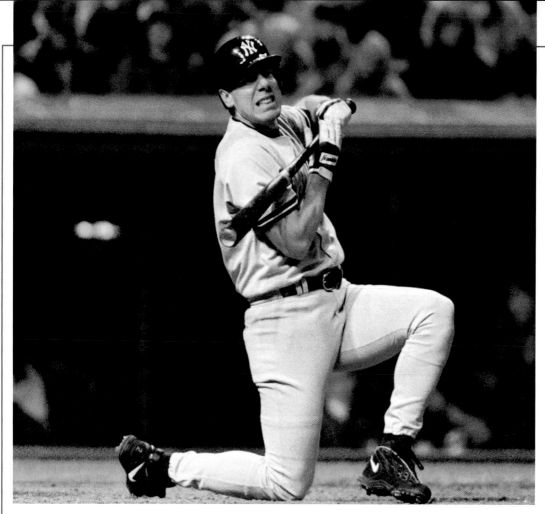

Pettitte's early exit (opposite) was only one reason for the New York defeat; Colon kept Yankees like Brosius (above) and Knoblauch (right) off balance all night, though Knoblauch did manage a pair of singles to atone somewhat for his Game 2 blunder.

Pettitte explained later that he felt too strong, after nine days of rest; that he felt he was overthrowing the ball and losing the usual movement on his pitches.

Thome launched a home run estimated at 421 feet leading off the second inning, and Mark Whiten ripped a double down the left-field line. Mel Stottlemyre trekked to the bullpen phone; Hideki Irabu began warming up. Enrique Wilson bounced a single through the Yankees' drawn-in infield, scoring Whiten, and Pettitte barely got through the second inning with Cleveland leading by only a run, at 2–1.

Pettitte was like a dazed fighter at that point, waiting to be knocked out, completely vulnerable.

But Torre and Stottlemyre decided to stick with him, give him a chance to fight through his problems, rather than call on Irabu to start the third inning. Somehow Pettitte got through the third and fourth innings unscathed, using a roundhouse curveball. The Yankees needed only to get him through the fifth with the score close, and then Torre could give the ball to Ramiro Mendoza.

Pettitte retired the first two hitters in the fifth. Just one more out.

"It looked like he had straightened himself out," Torre said, "and then in the fifth inning, it looked like he started muscling the ball a little bit."

With the count 0-1 on Manny Ramirez, Pettitte threw a fastball low and away, a good pitch, and Ramirez reached out and slammed the ball to right. Pettitte's head jerked as he watched the ball carry into the Yankees' bullpen in right field. Pettitte's body lurched in anger, as if he had taken a fist in the stomach.

And he folded quickly, yielding four or more runs in an inning for the 11th time this year, a major league high. Pettitte walked Fryman after getting ahead in the count, 0-2. Thome then lifted a long drive that landed on the top of the right-field wall and went over, before Whiten, a former Yankee, provided the coup de grace—a tremendous 416-foot drive that fell among the standing-room-only crowd far beyond the left-field wall.

Whiten flipped his bat gaudily, and Pettitte turned and dropped his head, devastated by the beating. He had never allowed four home runs in one game before.

As Torre emerged from the dugout to replace Pettitte with the score at 6–1, Cone and Wells, two of Pettitte's brethren, got up and walked into the runway, not wanting to see his departure. Talking softly to himself, Pettitte walked off the field, sat in the dugout, pulled on a jacket and got a cup of water.

Mendoza warmed up and Pettitte stared onto the field, straight ahead. Other Yankees approached him and tapped him on the leg or the side—as if to say, "Hang in there, man"—and Pettitte never reacted, his eyes never moved.

Pettitte would be among those who talked calmly later about a Yankees comeback. The Yankees are too good, Pettitte suggested, to lose this series. But the words did not match the expression on his face; the words of his teammates did not match their expressions, either.

"Everybody probably is a little bit angry with themselves," Girardi said. "We need to have better at-bats, we need to put better swings on pitches. When you get in situations like this, guys tend to try to do a little bit too much. We just need to get back to where you were and do what your part is."

Colon allowed a run in the first inning on a single by Knoblauch, a sacrifice bunt by Derek Jeter and a single by Bernie Williams. Colon was searching for control of some pitch other than his fastball; by the fifth inning, he had it, and the Yankees had no chance.

"We have to score," Jeter said. "We can't win if we can't score."

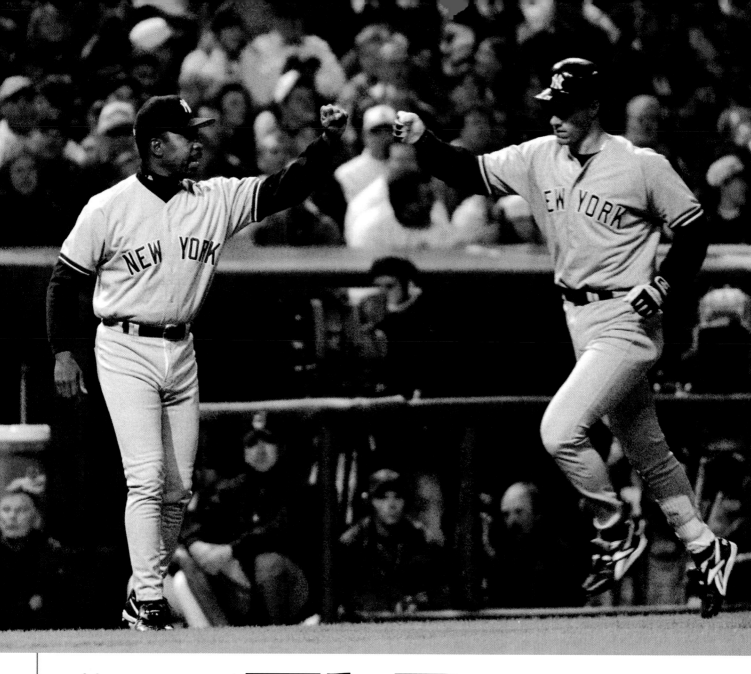

Game 4

El Duque to the Rescue

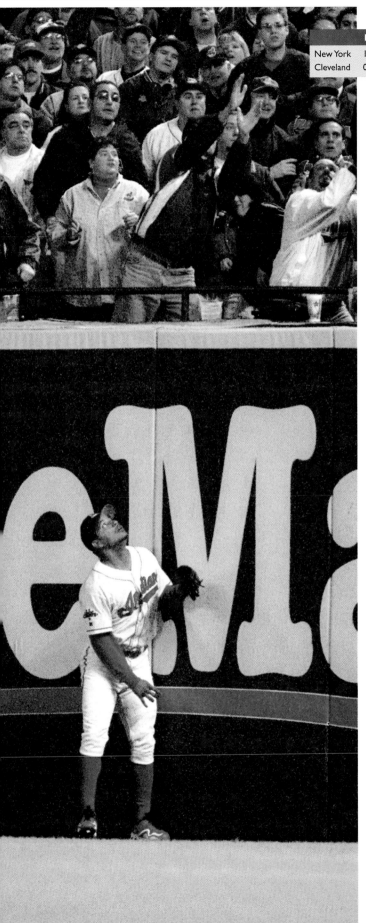

LINE SCORE										
New York	1	0	0	2	0	0	0	0	1	—4
Cleveland	0	0	0	0	0	0	0	0	0	—0

CLEVELAND—The Yankees spent recent years carefully piecing together their current juggernaut, but the player responsible for winning their most important game to date washed up on a sliver of island aboard a leaky boat last winter.

Orlando Hernández, the defector from Cuba, shut out the Cleveland Indians into the eighth inning tonight as the Yankees won, 4–0, and fought back to even the championship series at two games apiece.

Paul O'Neill hit a first-inning home run off the Indians' Dwight Gooden, and set up a second rally for the Yankees, whose collective slump continued; they scored their runs on just four hits. But they brightened the mood of their principal owner, George Steinbrenner, who called Hernández's outing "one of the best pitching performances I've ever seen."

Orlando and Livan Hernández are half brothers, with the same father and different mothers, and both got the big-game gene. Livan, a pitcher with the Florida Marlins, was the World Series most valuable player last year, winning two games against the Indians. Orlando took the ball last night in the most important game of the Yankees' season: a loss would have left them on the brink of playoff defeat and probable off-season chaos, as the front office tried to ascertain why a team that played almost perfectly in the regular season had been beaten by Cleveland again.

But Hernández carried himself this weekend as if there were no possibility he would lose. Relaxed and smiling perpetually when speaking with reporters, Hernández repeatedly referred to his escape from Cuba as he put his Game 4 start in perspective. After what he had survived, a journey with little food or water in a sea known to be a favored shark hangout, why would a baseball game bother him?

"I had pressure," he said after the game, "but I had no fear."

Hernández marched to the mound for the first inning, then stood at the rubber and paced off five small steps to locate his landing area for his front leg. He was ready to go to work, though he would have one great moment of anxiety almost immediately.

One out into the first inning, Omar Vizquel singled and stole second, and with two out, Manny Ramirez coaxed a walk from Hernández, who initially was having trouble controlling his sidearm slider. Jim Thome was next, 24 hours removed from his two-homer performance in Game 3, in a situation that Yankees Manager Joe Torre feared. If Hernández was going to run into trouble, Torre thought, it would be in the first few innings, when he was trying to find his command after not pitching for 15 games.

The count ran full, and Hernández threw a changeup, but the pitch drifted into Thome's danger zone. Thome smacked it with an uppercut, launching the ball toward the right-field seats on a parabolic trajectory, like so many home runs. The 44,981 patrons stood to follow the flight, roaring. "Off the bat," O'Neill said, "my heart dropped a little bit."

O'Neill (opposite, with third-base coach Willie Randolph) went deep with the game's 13th pitch, leaving Ramirez (left) nothing to do but watch helplessly as the ball soared into the stands.

Davis stroked a double to the opposite field to drive in the Yankees' second run.

But Thome had made contact near the end of his bat, and O'Neill moved back to the warning track and caught the ball just in front of the wall. The Yankees' slim 1–0 lead was intact. Said David Cone: "Who knows what that would've done to El Duque at that point? He was near perfect the rest of the way."

Their offense sputtering, the Yankees had needed a quick lift from somebody, some early-inning propulsion to take the pressure off. Thirteen pitches into the game, O'Neill waited on a low curveball from Gooden and golfed it into the right-field stands.

The Yankees did not exactly break out offensively after O'Neill's home run; they would collect just four hits all night, and they have just 26 in the four games of the series. But O'Neill's homer did

With the victory complete,
Hernández (opposite) received
happy hugs from his
fellow Yankees.

seem to apply pressure to Gooden, who pitched tentatively thereafter and set up the Yankees' fourth-inning rally himself.

Gooden walked O'Neill on six pitches to lead off the fourth, then walked Bernie Williams, as Cleveland Manager Mike Hargrove changed his posture uncomfortably in the dugout. Chili Davis leaned on a curveball and punched it into the left-field corner for what turned out to be a ground-rule double; O'Neill scored the Yankees' second run.

Tino Martinez lifted a high fly to center, of medium depth, and Williams retreated to third to tag up. But Kenny Lofton, Cleveland's center fielder, fumbled the ball as he removed it from his glove, and the second base umpire Jim McKean ruled no catch. Williams trotted home, uncontested, the Yankees' lead increasing to 3–0.

As Torre had predicted, Hernández's command improved as the game progressed. Said Hargrove, "I don't think he missed any spots all night."

In a loss to Cleveland in July, Hernández had stubbornly refused to pitch inside to left-handed hitters, but tonight he jammed them repeatedly, knocking them back off the plate before finishing them by flopping changeups low and away.

A single and a hit batter in the sixth gave Cleveland two on and one out, with Ramirez and Thome due to bat. But Hernández blew a fastball past Ramirez for strike three when Ramirez clearly was anticipating a breaking ball.

Jeff Nelson warmed up frantically in the Yankees' bullpen, unable to see the infield from his vantage point; he would replace Hernández, he knew, if Thome got a hit or a walk. But with a full count on Thome, Hernández flipped a changeup, Thome swung and Nelson heard the crowd groan. Hernández's teammates burst from the dugout to offer high-fives; some hugged each other. "He's obviously a big-game pitcher," Williams said.

Hernández's birthday is Sunday, and depending on whom you ask, he will turn 33 or 29 or something in between. But the Yankees do not care about the date on his birth certificate. They are only glad that he survived the sharks and drifted ashore in the Bahamas last December, and that he wears their uniform.

Another Step *Closer*

LINE SCORE										
New York	3	1	0	1	0	0	0	0	0	—5
Cleveland	2	0	0	0	0	1	0	0	0	—3

CLEVELAND—Forty-eight hours changed everything for the Yankees, 48 hours and two victories. Plummeting toward elimination after three games, the Yankees rediscovered the path of greatness: Edging the Cleveland Indians by 5–3 today, they took a lead of 3 games to 2 in the championship series.

The signs of vindication were all around. David Wells, taunted mercilessly by fans who referred to his deceased mother as he warmed up, pitched seven and one-third innings and dedicated the victory to his tormentors: "To those idiots out there, this one is for you." George Steinbrenner, who had been razzed by Cleveland fans during Game 3, playfully teased them before departing. David Cone, who left Jacobs Field with a stony glare after Game 3, dressed with a smile today, preparing to fly back to New York and pitch Game 6. Chuck Knoblauch, mocked by a cheering crowd here 48 hours ago, is grinning again after spurring a first-inning rally that the Indians would call the turning point of the game.

The Yankees were reeling after Game 3 and, as Steinbrenner said, "People were burying us." Now, with one more victory, the team seeking its own corridor in history will move on to the World Series.

The Yankees are operating with a distinct advantage in manpower now. Cleveland catcher Sandy Alomar suffered back spasms and was forced to leave Game 4. He did not start today, and may be finished for the series. And about two hours before today's game, outfielder David Justice approached Manager Mike Hargrove and asked out of the starting lineup, saying he wouldn't feel comfortable batting against the left-handed Wells.

Cleveland's lineup included three rookies—catcher Einar Diaz, first baseman Richie Sexson and second baseman Enrique Wilson. Chad Ogea, who was left off the Indians' roster in the 1997 division series against the Yankees, was on the mound against the Yankees' ace, Wells. Every aspect of this matchup favored the Yankees, who needed to seize control immediately.

Knoblauch, a favorite of the Cleveland fans since his mental mistake allowed the Indians to score the tie-breaking run in Game 2, led off for the Yankees and took two called strikes. Ogea then attempted to push Knoblauch away from the plate, but Knoblauch did not flinch, and the pitch bounced off his left side.

Derek Jeter struck out, admitting later that he barely saw Ogea's curveball in the late-afternoon shadows. These were not the type of conditions in which batters take full, comfortable swings. The Yankees felt compelled to press the action. "Any time a team gets a lead," Manager Joe Torre said,

Game 5

A solo home run by Davis (left) with two outs in the fourth inning gave the Yankees an insurmountable three-run lead.

OCTOBER 11, 1998 * YANKEES 5 * INDIANS 3

Wells responded to the taunts of the Cleveland fans with a sarcastic tip of his cap (left) and Rivera (right) slammed the door to seal the Yankee victory.

"you can afford to be a lot more aggressive."

With Paul O'Neill batting, Knoblauch broke from first base on a steal attempt, and shortstop Omar Vizquel began moving to cover second. O'Neill chopped a grounder that seemed destined for second base. "The ball was coming right at me," Vizquel said. "It was chest-high, no doubt a double play."

But Ogea jumped and reached for the bouncer. The ball glanced off his glove and past Vizquel into short left field, rolling far enough for Knoblauch to scamper to third base. Ogea could have been out of the inning. Instead, the Yankees had runners at first and third and one out. "That changed everything," Vizquel said. "The whole game turned at that moment."

Bernie Williams walked, filling the bases; Ogea's pitch total was at 18 and counting. He fell behind Chili Davis, 2 balls and 1 strike. Davis then turned on a low pitch and laced a grounder. Williams, leading off first, barely saw the bouncer heading directly at him. Williams started moving toward second, the ball bearing down on him. If he had been hit, he would have been out automatically, and the Yankees' rally would have been stunted. "I thought it was going to hit me for sure," Williams said. "I don't know how it missed me."

As Williams lifted his right foot, the ball skipped just under it, by a margin of perhaps half a shoelace. Then it ricocheted off Sexson's glove and into right field. Knoblauch scored, O'Neill scored and Williams charged to third.

Ogea hit Tino Martinez on the top of the foot with his next pitch, loading the bases again. Tim Raines grounded to second, with Cleveland's infield playing back, enabling Williams to rush across the plate. The Yankees led by 3–0, having received the initial burst of offense they needed, no matter how absurdly.

That gave Wells some room to absorb Cleveland's two runs in the bottom of the first. The Yankees scored single runs in the second and fourth innings, taking a 5–2 advantage, before Jim Thome banged his third home run of the series.

The situation became serious for the Yankees in the bottom of the eighth. Wells struck out Vizquel to lead off, his third consecutive strikeout. Wells, who sometimes throws 130 to 135 pitches, had reached 101. But with the right-handed-batting Travis Fryman coming up, Torre strolled to the mound to replace Wells. The pitcher was incredulous, complaining that he had made only one bad pitch.

When Wells's replacement, Jeff Nelson, hit Fryman with a fastball to bring the tying run to the plate, Wells violated protocol by stalking out of the dugout before the end of the inning. Manny Ramirez dumped a single in front of Raines, who was playing left field, driving the crowd of 44,966 into a comeback frenzy.

Torre replaced Nelson with the closer Mariano Rivera, and no doubt Wells was pacing somewhere in the Yankees' clubhouse—probably wondering, like many nervous Yankees fans, whether Torre had been guilty of over-managing.

But Rivera threw a sinking fastball and Mark Whiten bounced to second, where Knoblauch began an inning-ending double play.

Later, as the Yankees prepared to leave for New York, Steinbrenner walked into the bathroom, where Cone was shaving. "Ready, buddy?" Steinbrenner asked of his Game 6 starter. "We're going to kick some butt Tuesday."

In another 48 hours.

Chasing *the* Ghosts

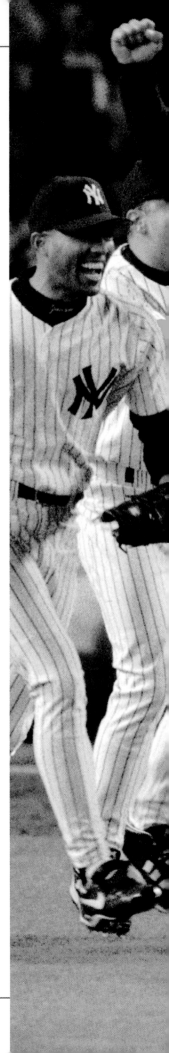

With the memory of their 1997 playoff failure against Cleveland now thoroughly erased, the Yankees celebrated yet another pennant.

Game 6

LINE SCORE				
Cleveland	0 0 0	0 5 0	0 0 0	—5
New York	2 1 3	0 0 3	0 0 X	—9

NEW YORK—Ghosts have hung over Yankee Stadium all season, David Cone once remarked, as the Yankees pursued their place among the greatest baseball teams in history. But it was ghosts of the very recent past that had haunted the Yankees this past week, until they won the American League championship tonight with a 9–5 victory over Cleveland.

The victory means that the Yankees will play in the World Series for the 35th time and the second time in three seasons. And it means they have exorcised the awful memory of their 1997 elimination by the Indians in the first round of the playoffs.

Trailing by 2 games to 1, the Yankees came back to win Games 4, 5 and 6 of this series, saving the Game 2 goat, Chuck Knoblauch, from the eternal disgrace that befell the likes of Fred Merkle and Bill Buckner.

Before 57,142 fans at Yankee Stadium, Scott Brosius hit a three-run homer, Derek Jeter stroked a two-run triple and Ramiro Mendoza and Mariano Rivera pitched flawless relief in a game in which the Yankees nearly blew a 6–0 lead.

When the game was over, when the players were damp and covered with the sweet smell of champagne, Jeter spotted a head of perfectly coiffed gray hair in the middle of the Yankees' clubhouse.

"Hold on," Jeter yelled out. "Hold on. Somebody's dry around here."

And with that, he reached and emptied a bottle of bubbly over George Steinbrenner, who flinched and laughed.

"I got him," Jeter said, escaping.

Inside the trainers' room, the Yankee players took turns shout-

OCTOBER 13, 1998 * YANKEES 9 * INDIANS 5

ing into a phone to Darryl Strawberry, their teammate who is recovering from surgery to remove a cancerous tumor from his colon. Knoblauch was among those who spoke to him before the game and after. We're thinking of you, Knoblauch told him, and Strawberry was probably thinking of Knoblauch.

The second baseman ignored the baseball in the Game 2 loss to argue a call as the decisive run scored, and throughout the 48-hour wave of hysteria that follows each playoff loss in New York, Knoblauch was a pariah. If the Yankees had lost the series, he would never have been forgiven.

But the Yankees took two of three games in Cleveland to take control of the series and Knoblauch had played well. When he was announced before his first plate appearance last night, many rose and cheered, as if to say, You're forgiven, for now.

"The hair on the back of my neck stood on end, to have them react to me that way," Knoblauch said later.

Knoblauch placed the Cleveland starter, Charles Nagy, on the defensive, fouling off a two-strike pitch, and then another and another, until Nagy had thrown nine pitches; even after Knoblauch grounded out to shortstop, a core of fans cheered him, understanding that he had chopped away a small piece of Nagy and given the Yankee hitters a chance to see what Nagy did or did not have.

Jeter chopped a roller toward third and hustled out a single. With the count 2-2 on Paul O'Neill, Jeter broke from first on a hit-and-run and O'Neill lined a curveball to right for a single, Jeter moving to third. Bernie Williams singled home one run and a sacrifice fly by Chili Davis scored another, and the Yankees had a 2–0 lead right away—the fifth time in the six games of this series they had scored in the first inning.

A double by Knoblauch helped produce another run in the second inning, and when Brosius launched his three-run homer to straightaway center field in the third inning—prefaced by umpire Ted Hendry's blown call that aided the Yankees—New York led, 6–0. Cone on the mound, no problem.

Cone imploded in the fifth, however. "I just lost it," he would say later. He allowed three straight hits (one of which hit Hendry on the backside, in another moment of ignominy for the umpire) and then a bases-loaded walk to force home a run. Cone struck out Manny Ramirez for the second out and the crowd roared. But Jim Thome blasted a titanic grand slam on Cone's next pitch, his fourth homer of the series, silencing Yankee Stadium. Just like that, the Indians had drawn to within a run, at 6–5.

But Cleveland's defense gave away three runs in the bottom of the sixth, an inning that began with the Gold Glove shortstop Omar Vizquel botching an easy throw to first. Girardi walked, and with one out Jeter launched a high drive to right-center. Ramirez charged back to the wall, looked up and leaped dramatically—as the ball landed at the base of the wall. Two runs scored, and Jeter would, as well, on another single from Williams.

Mendoza pitched three scoreless innings in relief of Cone, before Rivera closed out Cleveland in the ninth. When Rivera picked up Vizquel's grounder in the ninth and threw to first for the game's final out, the Yankees rushed from the dugout for the requisite hugs and head slaps and handshakes.

But they seemed subdued, more relieved than exhilarated. They kept their champagne spraying to a minimum, and nobody was dumping shaving cream or pudding on each other. Cone walked

Cone's disgusted reaction said it all after Thome's grand slam brought the Indians within a run at 6–5; Brosius (opposite, above) was the Yankees' hitting star, ripping a three-run homer in the third inning to put New York in front for good; after the victory, Torre (opposite below) shared a moment of celebration with his wife, Ali.

through the clubhouse carrying the championship trophy and was stopped by the voice of his manager. "Nice going, buddy," Joe Torre said to Cone, reaching out and hugging him; Torre had tears in his eyes, and as they looked at each other for an instant, Cone's lower lip quivered. They had overcome the ghosts of 1997.

"It's nice," Cone said, "to get past Cleveland after losing to them last year."

David Wells stood in front of his locker, slowly pulling the cork from a bottle. "There's another step to go," he said. "But there's a time and a place to party."

The World Series

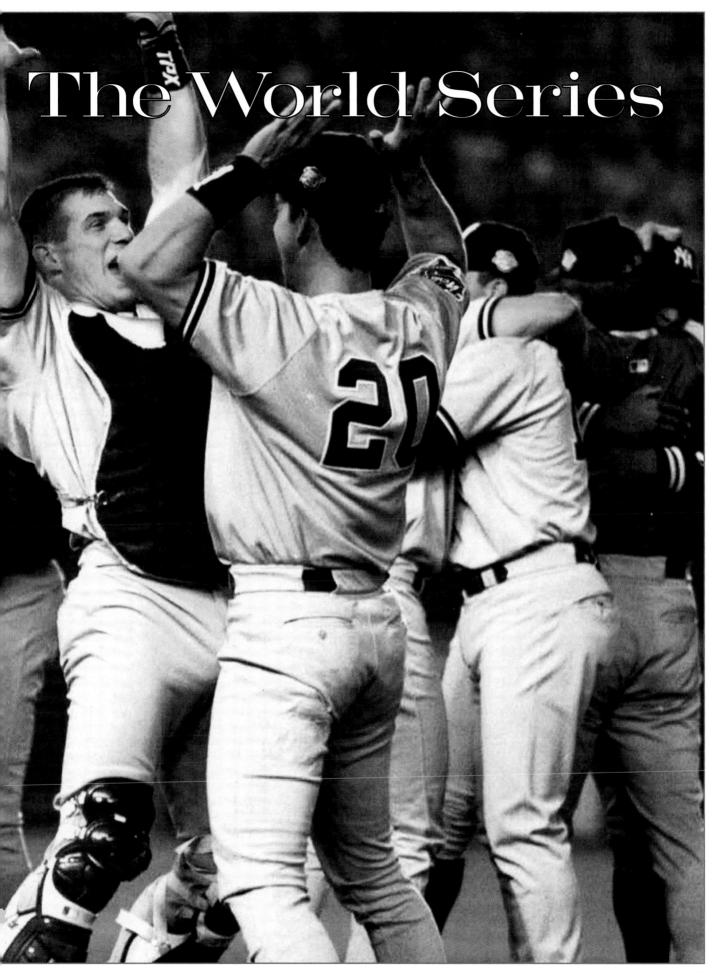

A Date With *Destiny*

The ever entertaining Wells (opposite) blithely predicted a Yankee victory in five games, then corrected himself later, proclaiming that New York would sweep; Brosius (left, hitting a home run in Game 2 of the division series) was more circumspect, expressing his respect for Brown's 97-m.p.h. sinking fastball.

BY BUSTER OLNEY

Until Orlando Hernández's victory over Cleveland in Game 4 of the American League Championship Series, the Yankees had played tensely in the post-season, almost desperately—and they got through. But as the A.L. playoffs ended and they prepared to play the San Diego Padres in the World Series, the Yankees were confident and loose. David Wells predicted on Howard Stern's radio show that the Yankees would win in five games, adding later that what he really should have said was that the Yankees would sweep the National League champions.

Wells's confidence had nothing to do with the caliber of the Padres, a veteran team that included Tony Gwynn, Greg Vaughn and Ken Caminiti, a team that had played extremely well in beating the Houston Astros and Atlanta Braves in the playoffs; Wells was very complimentary of the Padres. But after 114 victories in the regular season, a sweep of the Texas Rangers in the division series and then a six-game victory over Cleveland in the championship series, the Yankees had developed and deserved a sense of destiny. They were quite sure they were going to win.

Speaking generally of the Yankees, Joe Torre said: "They have this inner conceit about them—they know they're good, but they don't really care about telling other people how good they are. I'm impressed with that attitude.

"I've found out something in this post-season—that it's O.K. to be tense in games and admit that you're tense, and still do a good job. The determination is there. It's a terrific ball club when it comes to self-motivation and determination. This ball club is like no other club I've been around."

But they were all respectful and wary of the Padres and their ace, Kevin Brown, the Game 1 starter, who had the physical wherewithal to pitch and dominate three games in the series. The day before the series opened, Torre carried a thick red binder through the Yankees' clubhouse, holding it against his hip, like a mother with her child. The binder, as ample as any Yellow Pages, contained the Yankees' scouting report on the Padres. A section of the report addressed the past performances of Torre's hitters against the San Diego pitchers, and Torre could not have been encouraged by the numbers that illuminated Brown's dominance. Bernie Williams, the Yankees' cleanup batter, had just 4 hits in 17 at-bats against Brown, for a .235 average. Chili Davis was a career .170 hitter against the San Diego right-hander, Tino Martinez .118.

In fact, the only regular with a career average over .276 against Brown was third baseman Scott Brosius. And the Yankees had faced Brown when he pitched in the American League, before 1996, before he made improvements. "He throws a sinking fastball at about 97 miles per hour," Brosius said drolly. "That would make him a pretty good pitcher."

Said Torre: "Pitchers can dominate a game, no question. We know Kevin Brown is a good pitcher. Roger Clemens is a good pitcher. Pedro Martinez is a good pitcher. We just go out and try to do our thing. Hopefully, if he makes mistakes, we can take advantage of it."

And as they had all year, the Yankees wanted to make Brown work, they wanted to maintain patience in their at-bats, force him to throw a lot of pitches, perhaps knock him out in the sixth or seventh inning and give themselves a chance against the Padres' middle relief, the soft underbelly of any team. The Yankees took aim, with 121 victories in hand, and 4 to go.

The Yankees were hoping that Martinez (left, after striking out in Game 2 of the Division Series) and Williams (opposite), both of whom had been disappointing in the post-season, would find a way to be more productive against Brown and the Padres.

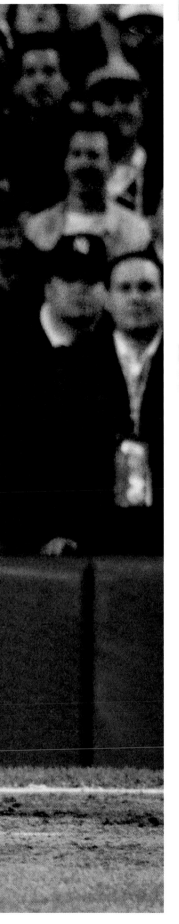

Seven in the Seventh

Game 1

LINE SCORE											
San Diego	0 0 2	0 3 0	0 1 0	—6
New York	0 2 0	0 0 0	7 0 X	—9

NEW YORK—The Yankees stalked San Diego's Kevin Brown in Game 1 of the World Series tonight, their pack of hitters relentlessly pressing and wearing him down, wearing him out. When Brown was finally driven from the mound, Chuck Knoblauch and Tino Martinez moved in for the kill.

The Yankees trailed by 5–2 in the seventh inning when Knoblauch launched a game-tying three-run homer. Five batters later, Martinez—a benign post-season hitter for the last three years—crushed a grand slam. The seven-run explosion rocketed the Yankees to a 9–6 victory.

Beyond seizing the early advantage in the Series, the Yankees managed to neutralize Brown, widely seen as San Diego's best chance to prevail. Brown, perhaps the most dominant right-hander in the majors, could pitch in as many as three games before the World Series is over. But now he can only win in two, if he gets the chance.

With the Yankees ahead by 2–0 in the third inning, the Padres' Greg Vaughn slammed a two-run home run off David Wells. Then, with two outs in the fifth, Wells's post-season invincibility completely abandoned him. Three straight pitches: a broken-bat single by Quilvio Veras, a two-run homer by Tony Gwynn, another home run by Vaughn. Wells turned away in dismay as Vaughn's home run crashed into the left-field stands. Yankee Stadium was silent, nary a cry of Ansky.

"He missed spots," Joe Torre later said of Wells.

All the while, however, the Yankees had slowly surrounded Brown. Chili Davis had whacked a single off Brown's shin in the second inning, and though Brown continued to pitch, Davis felt certain he had hit the ball hard enough to hurt the pitcher. Brown, already hampered by a sinus infection, went to three-ball counts on six of the next eight hitters. He threw 32 pitches in the second inning, 20 more in the third, 64 in all in the first three

Mired in a horrible post-season slump, Martinez broke out with a mammoth grand slam in the seventh inning that gave the Yankees a 9–5 lead.

OCTOBER 17, 1998 * YANKEES 9 * PADRES 6

innings. He would run out of gas; the Yankees were sure about that. It was just a matter of when.

"We needed to make him throw a lot of pitches," Davis said. "We needed to make him tired."

Brown retired the first batter in the bottom half of the seventh, before Jorge Posada hit a single. The talk in the Yankees' dugout picked up, Homer Bush remembered later. Brown walked the rookie Ricky Ledee, who had doubled in the second inning to drive in Davis and Martinez; Brown's pitches were now sailing out of the strike zone. He had reached 108 pitches in only six and one-third innings, and he was finished, relieved by Donne Wall, with Knoblauch coming to bat.

This is what the Yankees have done all year: force a starter from the game in the middle innings, before exploiting middle relievers.

Wall appeared nervous, throwing a head-high fastball to Knoblauch to fall behind in the count, two balls and no strikes. Wall had to throw a strike, and Knoblauch swung hard, lifting a high fly down the left-field line. Off the bat, it did not look like much, leaving the 56,712 fans murmuring. Then the murmurs became shouts, and the shouts became screams as the ball drifted closer to the stands, Vaughn backing toward the wall.

"I had a pretty good feeling," Knoblauch said, "until I saw Vaughn at the wall." But Vaughn backed up, leaped and watched the ball disappear. Tie game. Yankee Stadium shook. Knoblauch triple-jumped around the bases, crossed home plate and thrust both arms into the air, yelling to the crowd like a hyped Olympic weight lifter who had just hoisted a half-ton. He stomped around the dugout, his helmet on, teammates banging on him happily.

"I just got caught up in the excitement of the moment," Knoblauch said later.

Derek Jeter singled amid the screams, and nobody really noticed. Wall left the game, and Mark Langston took over.

Paul O'Neill flied out, and after Jeter advanced on a wild pitch, Bernie Williams was intentionally walked, and Davis worked a walk against Langston, a longtime teammate when both were with the California Angels.

Bases loaded once more, with Martinez due to hit; Martinez, with exactly one r.b.i. in his 76 career at-bats in league championship and World Series games. Chris Chambliss, the Yankees' hitting coach, watched and hoped that the fact that Langston was left-handed would force Martinez to keep his proper mechanics, keep his front shoulder in and stay on top of the ball. "This is your time," a teammate yelled to Martinez from the Yankees' dugout, others echoing the words.

With the count two balls and two strikes, Langston threw a fastball near the outside corner, so close that the players on the Yankees' bench went silent. A strike, Langston thought. The pitch that would end the inning, he thought. It could have been a strike or a ball, the San Diego pitching coach, Dave Stewart, said later.

Rich Garcia, the home plate umpire, called it a ball. Langston glared, snapping at the return throw. Langston and Martinez and everyone on the field now understood that with the bases loaded and a 3–2 count, Langston would have to throw what players refer to as a cookie—a tasty pitch over the middle.

"I was looking for a fastball," Martinez said.

Martinez ate up this cookie. The ball soared into the upper deck in right field, a grand slam, lifting three years of post-season misery off the back of the Yankees' first baseman. "I knew that eventually, I'd come up in a big situation and get a big hit to help the team win," Martinez said.

After he returned to the dugout, the crowd called Martinez out again. Like Knoblauch, Martinez pumped both arms, and later the crowd would chant his name, and Martinez waved his cap. San Diego's lead was long gone, their best pitcher was gone, their relievers were beaten, victims of pin-striped stalkers.

After his three-run shot drifted out of Vaughn's reach (opposite) to tie the game, Knoblauch reacted with an intense celebration (above).

Always on the Attack

Game 2

LINE SCORE											
San Diego	0	0	0	0	1	0	0	2	0	—3
New York	3	3	1	0	2	0	0	0	X	—9

NEW YORK—The San Diego Padres, champions of the National League, have looked an awful lot like doormats against the Yankees in the World Series. But then, so does every other team the Yankees play.

The post-season was supposed to provide the ultimate test of greatness. Instead, the Yankees are treating it like extra credit. They crushed San Diego, 9–3, in Game 2 tonight at Yankee Stadium to take a 2–0 lead in the series. Orlando Hernández allowed a run in seven innings, the only run he has permitted in 14 innings in the post-season.

The Yankees and Padres will resume the series two days from now in San Diego, with little reason to believe San Diego can mount a comeback, other than the fact that they arrived on time for the first two games.

"We've got two more games to win," George Steinbrenner said. "And it ain't going to be easy." Or maybe it will, for the Padres are a mess. Sterling Hitchcock, scheduled to start Game 3 against the Yankees' David Cone, has flu-like symptoms. Andy Ashby started tonight without a voice and with a sore throat and head cold, and he would leave the field with this pitching line: two and two-thirds innings, 10 hits, 7 runs (4 earned), 1 walk and 1 strikeout.

Everybody has looked bad against the Yankees this year. They have won 9 of 11 playoff games, and have nearly doubled their post-season opponents' run production, 54–30. Joe Torre believes they have won 123 games this year largely because they have respected all their opponents, taken them all

OCTOBER 18, 1998 * YANKEES 9 * PADRES 3

O'Neill's running grab (opposite) in the first inning robbed Wally Joyner of an extra-base hit, just one reason the San Diego dugout (above) was as glum as the Yankee fans were gleeful.

seriously. They beat up the expansion Tampa Bay Devil Rays and now are beating up the Padres, who appear powerless against them.

"The approach isn't different," Derek Jeter said. "This team doesn't like to lose. Everybody keeps the same approach and the same intensity level against everybody."

The Yankees wasted no time in attacking Ashby and the Padres, exploiting a gamble made by San Diego Manager Bruce Bochy. Knowing that left-handed batters hit 109 points higher than right-handed batters against Hernández this year, Bochy inserted the left-handed-hitting Greg Myers into his lineup at catcher, in Myers's first start since Sept. 17.

Right away, Myers failed to catch a foul pop hit by the lead-off batter Chuck Knoblauch, who then walked. Myers throws poorly, so Knoblauch swiped second and established that the Yankees would run aggressively. Paul O'Neill chopped a grounder to third, and when Ken Caminiti threw high and wide, Knoblauch scored. Then O'Neill broke for second on a ground ball back to the mound; if he had not been running, if Myers had not been catching, the play might have led to an inning-ending double play.

Then came successive hits by Chili Davis, Tino Martinez and Scott Brosius, and the Yankees led, 3–0.

Knoblauch stole second in the first inning as the Yankees continued to keep the pressure on the Padres' pitching staff.

Ashby, nursing his cold and sore throat, needed quick innings. He needed a chance to retreat to the clubhouse, to catch his breath, to review the innings past and ahead. But the Yankees treated him the same way they treated Kevin Brown in Game 1, taking pitches, making Ashby work, wearing him down.

The Yankees sent 14 batters to the plate in the first two innings, and only O'Neill swung at the first pitch, in each of his two at-bats. Ashby threw 29 pitches to get through that first inning and needed almost as many in the second. "He went back out for the second," Bochy said, "and he didn't have quite the same stuff."

Ricky Ledee, who reached base in his first seven plate appearances in this Series, led off the second with a single and Knoblauch walked. Myers threw out Ledee at third on an attempted double steal, but Jeter hit a run-scoring single. Two batters later, Bernie Williams leaned on Ashby, fouling off three two-strike pitches; it was like watching a cat toy with a beleaguered mouse.

Finally, Ashby threw a sinking fastball, his 50th pitch of the night, and Williams drove it into the right-field stands for a two-run home run—in what could have been Williams's last game as a Yankee at the Stadium. (Williams is eligible for free agency after this season, and he will entertain offers from other teams that are expected to be higher than what the Yankees most likely will bid.)

The Yankees applied the coup de grace to Ashby in the third, Ledee driving in another run, and Bochy went out to get his pitcher.

As baseball lore has it, the 1927 Yankees—heretofore considered by many to be the greatest team of all time—all but defeated the Pittsburgh Pirates in the World Series when they took batting practice. The burly sluggers Babe Ruth and Lou Gehrig smashed monstrous drives as the Pirates, diminutive in comparison, supposedly stood nearby and gawked, psychologically beaten.

Their expressions could not have been much different than the one on Ashby's face after Bochy took him out in the third inning.

The Yankees led, 7–0, and Hernández was in complete control, throwing fastballs when it appeared the Padres were anticipating his curveball, flipping changeups when batters were thinking fastball. Only three times in the first six innings did a Padres base runner reach scoring position. By the seventh inning, this felt nothing like a World Series game and every bit like a midseason blowout against Detroit. Fans departed early; those who stayed cheered the former Yankees catcher Jim Leyritz when he was announced as a pinch-hitter, and Torre used the last innings to get work for his relievers.

Torre said that the Yankees' comeback against Atlanta in the 1996 World Series will be a reminder that any Series can turn around quickly, that a 2–0 advantage does not necessarily translate into a title. But there is a sense of inevitability about San Diego's fate.

Not exactly a fall classic. To be precise, this classic began in the spring in Tampa and may reach its zenith this week in San Diego.

After fouling off three two-strike pitches, Williams hit a two-run homer to give New York a 6–0 lead in the second inning.

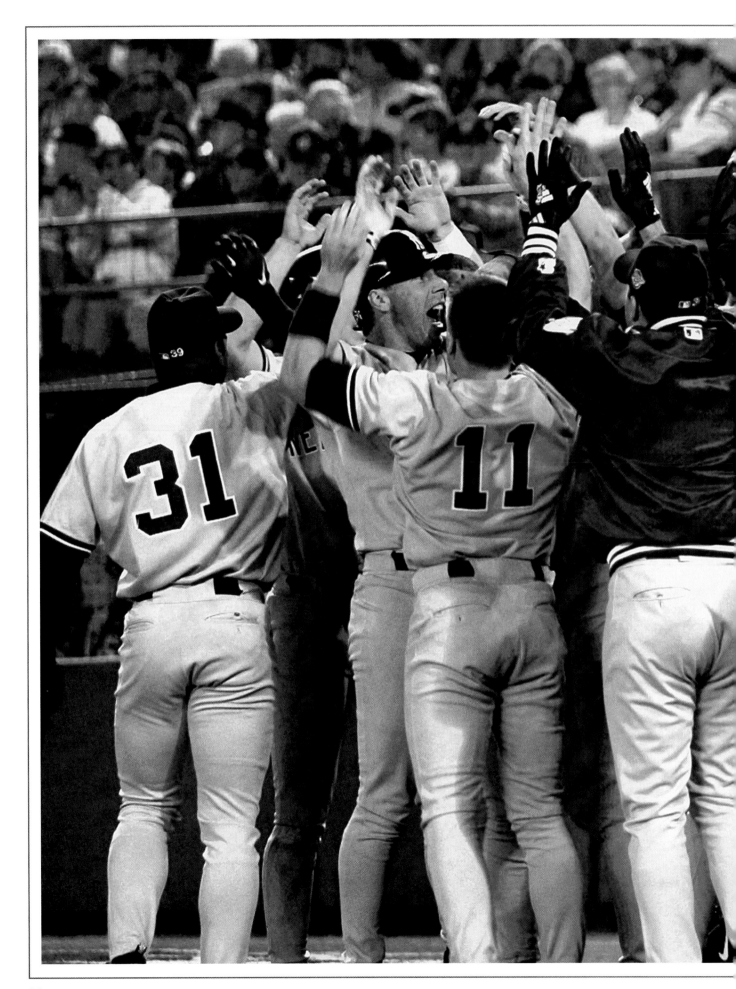

The *Glint* in Brosius' Eye

Game 3

LINE SCORE						
New York	0 0 0	0 0 0	2 3 0	—5
San Diego	0 0 0	0 0 3	0 1 0	—4

SAN DIEGO—The day before the playoffs began, David Cone was asked to pick one Yankee who might shine in the post-season.

"Scott Brosius," Cone replied, adding, "He's got that glint in his eye."

And so he does. Brosius, who hit a home run in Game 6 of the championship series, slugged two more tonight, including a three-run shot in the eighth inning that gave the Yankees a 5–4 victory over San Diego in the first World Series game here in 14 years. The homer also gave the Yankees a commanding lead of three games to none. No team has ever come back from that deficit to win the final four games of a World Series.

"This is the type of thing that you've dreamt about as a kid," Brosius said. "I've done this in my backyard a hundred times."

But this was the first time in the World Series, with 64,667 fans screaming at him, hoping he would fail, hoping the Padres would hang on to a 3–2 lead in the eighth inning and give themselves a chance to even the Series in Game 4 tomorrow night.

The Yankees had been fighting uphill all night, it seemed. Cone started and had not allowed a hit in the first five innings, but he acknowledged later that he had been laboring.

He managed to find a way. Between innings, Cone would throw his first warm-up tosses lightly, stiffly, like a 10-year-old trying to throw a snowball while wearing three sweaters and a parka. With the long commercial delays between innings, most

Brosius' three-run home run in the eighth—his second long ball of the night—put the Yankees in front for good.

OCTOBER 20, 1998 * YANKEES 5 * PADRES 4

pitchers throw 12 to 15 warm-ups. Cone rarely threw one or two more warm-ups beyond the typical allotment of eight.

His stuff seemed quite ordinary, his first fastballs clocked at 87 to 88 miles an hour, and Cone seemed unable to command his fastballs consistently; he threw only 53 percent of his pitches for strikes. After Tony Gwynn's first at-bat, in which he lined out to left field, he returned to the dugout and told the Padres' hitting coach, Merv Rettenmund, that Cone did not have a good fastball, and Rettenmund agreed.

In a scoreless game, Cone led off the Yankees' sixth with his third hit in eight career at-bats in the World Series, and the Yankees eventually had the bases loaded and one out against Sterling Hitchcock. But Bernie Williams struck out and Tino Martinez popped out, ending the inning.

After having spent a half-inning running the bases, Cone allowed a leadoff single to Hitchcock—turnabout—and a walk to Quilvio Veras, "the key to the inning," Cone would say later. Gwynn pulled a

Cone (above), who pitched well in spite of not having his best stuff, had predicted that Brosius (opposite, hitting a solo home run in the seventh) would be the man to watch in the Series.

Knoblauch beat out a bunt for a single in the sixth, when the Yankees loaded the bases but failed to score.

single through the right side, and when the inning was over, San Diego led, 3–0.

But Brosius led off the Yankee seventh with a home run, spurring a two-run rally that had the Yankees trailing by 3–2 in the eighth inning, with San Diego intent on delivering a lead into the hands of its dominating closer, Trevor Hoffman.

With the left-handed-hitting Paul O'Neill leading off the eighth for the Yankees, Padres Manager Bruce Bochy elected to start the inning with the left-hander Randy Myers on the mound. Myers walked O'Neill, putting the tying run on base, and Bochy then called for Hoffman, who converted 53 of 54 save opportunities and allowed only two home runs during the regular season. The Qualcomm Stadium crowd roared, the loudest that Yankees Manager Joe Torre said he had ever heard from a crowd, anywhere, any time.

But it was apparent immediately that Hoffman, who had not thrown in a game in six days, was pitching at less than his best. Typically, Hoffman throws a fastball at 92 to 94 m.p.h. His first fastball to Bernie Williams tonight was clocked at 88 m.p.h., and Williams drove a pitch to the base of the wall in right field, where it was caught, a 355-foot out.

When Williams returned to the dugout, he mentioned to teammates that he had been out in front of Hoffman's fastball, and word was passed down the line. With Martinez batting, Hoffman began pitching passively, throwing his slider and his changeup, and Martinez also drew a walk. Dave Stewart, San Diego's pitching coach, went to the mound. From the stands, Yankee scouts noticed that Hoffman wasn't throwing his changeup for strikes, as he usually does.

Brosius was the next batter, having gotten a late briefing from the hitting coach Chris Chambliss: His changeup is his best pitch, Chambliss reminded Brosius. Changeup, fastball.

Brosius couldn't remember for sure, but he thought he had faced Hoffman in this year's All-Star Game.

His arm packed in ice, Cone stood in the middle of the visitors' clubhouse and watched Brosius bat on television, like the rest of the world. Two runners on base, the Yankees down a run.

Brosius tried checking his swing unsuccessfully on the first pitch, a ball in the dirt, then took two more off-speed pitches for balls; later, Hoffman would lament the fact that he had thrown a slider out of the strike zone and fallen behind in the count.

Hoffman threw a fastball, 89 m.p.h., and Brosius fouled it off.

Hoffman came back at him with another fastball, 91 m.p.h. Brosius swung, and on the television screen Cone watched, the ball soared directly toward the lens. Oh, my, Cone said he was thinking—is that going to make it?

The Yankees' players leaped off their bench to follow the ball's flight. Go, go, some yelled, as San Diego center fielder Steve Finley ran back to the wall, Hoffman staring at the numbers on the back of Finley's jersey. When the ball carried over the fence, Brosius thrust both arms into the air halfway between first and second base.

San Diego scored a run in the bottom of the eighth, shaving the lead to 5–4, and back-to-back singles gave them two on with two out in the ninth inning—the tying run at third, the potential winning run at first.

But Mariano Rivera blew a high fastball past the swinging Andy Sheets to end the game on a strikeout, and the Yankees burst from their dugout once more, rushing to hug Rivera, and Brosius, with the glint in his eye.

One hundred and twenty-four down. One to go.

Game 4
A Team Like No Other

LINE SCORE					
New York	0 0 0	0 0 1	0 2 0	—3
San Diego	0 0 0	0 0 0	0 0 0	—0

SAN DIEGO—The Yankees have been a team greater than the sum of its parts all year, and when they secured their own place in history tonight, it was appropriate that a pitcher who had struggled in recent weeks pushed them there.

Andy Pettitte, dropped to the back of the Yankees' rotation for the World Series, applied the final piece to their mosaic, pitching seven and a third shutout innings and outdueling Kevin Brown in a 3–0 victory. In achieving their first Series sweep since 1950 and the seventh in their history, the Yankees wrapped up their 24th championship. They finished the year with 125 victories and 50 losses in the regular season and post-season combined, shattering the previous record of 118.

Scott Brosius, named the most valuable player in the Series, sensed as the ninth inning began that he would make the final play, and so it was: The Padres pinch-hitter Mark Sweeney grounded to third base, and after Brosius threw to first for the final out, he raised his hands into the air. Mariano Rivera, the Yankees' closer, dropped to his knees near the mound, and the other Yankees piled around. Chuck Knoblauch, the smallest Yankee, was lifted off his feet over and over.

Then they retreated to their clubhouse to spray each other with champagne—the good stuff, as promised by George Steinbrenner.

"This is as good as any team I've ever had," Steinbrenner said, his hair slick. "This is as good as any team that's ever played the game."

David Wells, the pitcher who threw a perfect game in May, pronounced this team the greatest ever. "Maybe someone will come along and beat our record," Wells said. "But this is history."

Players gathered to hoist bottles and chant the name of Darryl Strawberry, who was recovering at his New Jersey home following the removal of a cancerous tumor. With the clubhouse packed, many

With the Series-clinching victory in the bag, the Yankees began some serious celebrating; among the delirious New Yorkers were (from left to right, beginning on opposite page): Rivera and Joe Girardi, Williams (above), Wells (below), a jumble of Yankees, and the Series m.v.p. Brosius.

then went back onto the field to yell and scream and hug again. Tino Martinez, cigar in hand, walked to the mound with his wife at his side and saluted the brigade of Yankees fans who gathered above the visitors' dugout. Pettitte grabbed teammates and thanked them. "I tend to think about the bad things," Pettitte said. "So this is definitely very gratifying for me."

Pettitte beat Kevin Brown, the San Diego ace, who began the game firing like a gunfighter. Throwing a variety of fastballs that ranged from 88 to 96 miles per hour, Brown dominated the Yankees early, needing only 45 pitches to get through the first four innings.

Pettitte was far less overpowering, but no less effective, and he donned his own peculiar stare—hat curled low as if to hide his eyes, mouth turned down, shoulders square.

Pitching to San Diego's Quilvio Veras in the bottom of the first inning, Pettitte threw a sinking fastball low and away—a pitch that had not been called a strike in Game 3 of the championship series, when Cleveland pounded him for four home runs. Tonight Dana DeMuth, the home plate umpire, said strike 1, and Pettitte had a target that he would throw to time and again. He would get 17 groundball outs, shutting out the Padres into the eighth.

The Yankees broke through in the sixth, with one out. Jeter hit a high bouncer toward shortstop and, running hard all the way as he always does, easily beat the throw from Chris Gomez. O'Neill, his World Series batting average hovering barely above .100, turned on a low fastball and pulled it into the right-field corner, the ball skidding on the hard outfield and reaching the wall. Jeter raced around second, turned at third and stopped. With one out, the Padres' infield came in, attempting to prevent Jeter from scoring the game's first run.

Bernie Williams, who acknowledged before the game that this might be his last with the Yankees, swung fully and bounced a high chopper off the plate, toward the pitcher's mound; moving on con-

tact, Jeter broke from third. Brown waited for the chopper to come down, then leaped and reached with his right hand to grab the ball.

Brown glanced homeward, but Jeter was already knocking catcher Carlos Hernandez off his feet with a slide across home, and Brown had to settle for an out at first. The Yankees scored 965 runs in the regular season and another 59 in their first 12 games of the post-season. This particular run had the potential to bring them the crown they sought since reporting to spring training.

The Yankees added two runs in the top of the eighth against Brown on two walks and two hits, including a run-scoring single that Brosius lofted softly over the head of the drawn-in shortstop. When the top of the inning was over, Brown walked off the field and sarcastically tipped his cap to an umpire, upset over an earlier call and defiant to the end.

The Yankees then had to survive one last scare in the bottom of the eighth. Pettitte walked Veras and allowed a single to Tony Gwynn with one out, and the crowd of 65,427—the largest ever to see a baseball game in this city—screamed together, hoping for a comeback. Jeff Nelson relieved Pettitte and whiffed Greg Vaughn, but when he fell behind Ken Caminiti, two balls and no strikes, Torre called for Rivera.

Caminiti lined a single to right field, loading the bases, and Jim Leyritz, the former Yankee with a taste for cowboy boots and a penchant for post-season home runs, ambled to the plate. But Leyritz lined out to Williams, an out that effectively finished the Padres and guaranteed the Yankees their legacy.

Later, Jeter, his shirt and face wet from champagne, held a bottle in one hand and a cigar in the other. "I'm a little young to know about the teams back in the early 1900s," said the 24-year-old Jeter, "but we were 125 and 50, and there's not too many teams that can say that."

Just one.

The brilliant performance by Pettitte (opposite, above), who shut the Padres out for 7⅓ innings, erased the sour taste of his previous start in the ALCS; one fan (opposite, below) thought Brosius was ready for a different kind of contest; even hard-bitten veterans like Steinbrenner (above, left) and Torre got a bit emotional with the championship trophy in their hands.

The Celebration

The joyous ticker-tape parade up New York's lower Broadway (right) drew some 3.5 million fans, more than a few as high-spirited as the demonstrative duo below.

The Yankee family was out in force, including Joe Torre and George Steinbrenner (above, left and right, respectively); Darryl Strawberry (left); David Wells (below, shooting his own video of the crowd); and Andy Pettitte and David Cone (bottom, left and right, respectively).

Yankee People

Do You Believe This?

NEW YORK, Oct. 16 — David Wells was one of the last players in the clubhouse after the Yankees eliminated the Indians and danced into the World Series on Tuesday night, still jabbering and finding out where the team was going to celebrate. Suddenly he stopped talking and started cursing. He had problems. His blue jeans were wet.

Wells had asked one of the clubhouse kids to wash his jeans and hang them in his locker to dry overnight, but they were still damp.

"They're not dry," Wells said incredulously.

The teen-age attendant, his eyes wider than baseballs, said, "But they were hung there all night."

Offering a devilish grin, Wells said: "I know. Do you believe this?"

It is a question that is often, and appropriately, asked about Wells—about his wildly successful season, his once sporadic and now soaring career and his interesting 35 years on this and any other planet. Do you believe this?

His nickname is Boomer, which is perfect for a guy who says and does whatever he wants and whatever makes people notice him, who weighs 245 pounds, is going bald and has a veritable family album of tattoos etched across his body. It has always been easy to focus on Wells's excessive girth, his relaxed attitude and his carefree life style and forget that he is a very talented pitcher. Not anymore. Not after this season.

Wells, never one to hide his emotions, proved in 1998 that he was capable of battling—and winning—even without his finest stuff.

"I haven't stopped to think about all of this yet," he admitted. "I will, though. It's something we've played for all year, trying to get to this point. Now we're here and I don't know what to do."

So much has happened for Wells this season. The perfect game in May. A close-to-perfect 18–4 regular season. A 3–0 record so far in the post-season. Wells rose up; he got tougher when situations got tenser and he is the best pitcher on the best team in baseball.

For everyone except Wells, it is easy to recall the moment when he became a more determined pitcher and no longer an occasional quitter: May 17, the gorgeous day when Wells watched 27 Minnesota Twins amble to the plate and trudge back to the dugout. Boomer was carried off the field like a hero by his teammates and has not stopped piloting them since.

Joe Torre, who has been the disciplined father to Wells's rebellious son, has praised him more since the perfect game than he did all last season.

"I think he's a tougher pitcher now because he battles," Torre said. "He demands more from himself. He's always had great stuff, but he'd never gone beyond that. If it was a bad day for him, he accepted it. Now he won't accept it."

Not surprisingly, the proud Wells does not believe there has been a transformation. If he agreed, that would mean he had underachieved in the past.

"The only thing that has changed since the perfect game is my life style," snapped Wells, who went 14–3 with a 3.02 e.r.a. from the day of the perfect game until the end of the season. "I can't go to as many places. But I haven't changed as a pitcher."

—*JACK CURRY*

The Squeals of the Crowd

NEW YORK, Sept. 4—Whenever Derek Jeter's name is announced, whenever he gets another pivotal hit or makes another slick fielding play, the reaction is different than it is for other Yankees. For others at Yankee Stadium, there are roars. For Jeter, there are squeals. They escalate as if he were a singer with the Backstreet Boys.

The young fans, especially the young girls, marvel at Jeter. They adore him because he is young and handsome, because he plays shortstop for the Yankees and because he chats with them from the on-deck area.

But do not let the squealing obscure how important Jeter is to the Yankees. Even the smartest baseball scout might squeal after watching him play. The 24-year-old Jeter may be as valuable a player as the record-setting Yankees have.

Of course, that raises another question. If Jeter is the most valuable Yankee—and it is probably either Jeter or Bernie Williams—could he also be the most valuable player in the American League? There are several worthwhile candidates, including Williams, Boston's Nomar Garciaparra or Mo Vaughn and Texas's Juan Gonzalez. Still, Jeter belongs in the discussion.

Jeter usually handles questions about personal accomplishments by looking at his feet, saying something about not being perfect until he bats 1.000 and makes no errors and shifting the focus to the team. He has been this modest since his rookie season in 1996. But Jeter embraced a discussion about the m.v.p. award long enough to lobby for his type of player.

"It's flattering to have your name mentioned," said Jeter. "I'm not going to hit 50 homers or have 180 r.b.i.'s. Not too many people can do that. But you can work on the little things and the things that are valuable to your team. For me, it's moving a guy over, bunting and playing defense. A lot of people look at homers and r.b.i.'s as the only thing that's important, and that's not true."

When Joe Torre was asked about the m.v.p., the first name he mentioned was Jeter, then Williams.

"What makes it tough with our ball club is we've had so many players contribute, there will be a splitting of the votes," Torre said. "All of a sudden, the guy with the best numbers gets it."

Ask Jeter what he needs to improve on and he responds like a high school senior addressing a college coach. He wants to run the bases better, reduce his strikeouts, boost his on-base percentage, cut down on his errors and belt 30 homers. Most important, the m.v.p. candidate wants to continue hearing squeals until the Yankees win another ring.

"The only way we can have a better season than when we won the World Series in 1996 is to do it again," Jeter said. "Regardless of what we do in the regular season, unless we win the World Series again, it's not going to be very rewarding."

—*JACK CURRY*

Jeter, often the first out of the dugout to congratulate a teammate (opposite), is not too modest to acknowledge the cheers himself every once in a while (above).

An Empty Place

NEW YORK, Aug. 12—Orlando Hernández won his second major league start on June 9, beating Montreal, 11–1, in the first affirmation of his ability. Hernández returned to the visitors' clubhouse in Olympic Stadium, sat in a chair at his locker, his back turned to his teammates, and he began to cry.

Nobody was quite sure what to say, and few understood why Hernández was crying. José Cardenal, the Yankees' first-base coach, quietly explained it to Joe Torre and others: Hernández, who defected from Cuba last December, badly misses his children, 7-year-old Yahumara and 2-year-old Steffi, girls born during Hernández's first marriage. He wishes they could be in the United States with him, wishes they could see him in his new life.

"It's very hard for him," said Cardenal, who, like Hernández, is a native of Cuba. "He loves his family, and there is nothing he can do."

Hernández is expressive and gregarious, reaching up to tap an acquaintance on the shoulder when he passes, a greeting in any language. Even when speaking Spanish through an interpreter, Hernández will look his questioner directly in the eye, generally punctuating his answers with a smile.

But when Cardenal first interpreted a question today about Hernández's two daughters, the pitcher turned and looked down, his run-on answers reduced to a single sentence or a word or two.

Hernández said he speaks to his daughters by telephone as often as he can. He tries not to dream about them, or think about the situation. Being away from them is very hard. Yahumara was named after a dear friend, he explained. Steffi was named after the tennis player Steffi Graf.

Hernández's face brightened when he was asked about their personalities. Yahumara is quiet, he said, like most children her age. Steffi is "a fireball," Cardenal said, interpreting. "She doesn't like to take orders."

So, Steffi's favorite word is "No"?

"Si," Hernández said. His smile was brief. And then he was off to work out.

Hernández's younger brother Livan pitches for the Florida Marlins, and there are branches of family and friends from Cuba he could come to know. But Cardenal wonders how Hernández will cope during the off season, when there will be no baseball to distract him from the thoughts and memories of his daughters.

—*BUSTER OLNEY*

Yahumara and Steffi, along with Hernández's mother and his former wife, were granted permission by the Cuban Government to come to the United States to attend the Yankees' victory parade in Manhattan two days after the end of the World Series—10 months after Hernández fled Cuba.

Already a Survivor

ARLINGTON, Tex., Oct. 1—"Hey, Skip." This was behind the batting cage at noon on a Sunday in Montreal, during the pennant race of September 1984, back when the Mets were young and Darryl Strawberry was going to hit 1,000 home runs.

Strawberry and Davey Johnson went off in a corner and had a terse little conversation, and pretty soon Strawberry was out of the lineup, not up to playing so soon after whatever he had been doing on Saturday night. I remember one of the Mets' coaches banging his fungo bat against the batting cage.

That was a Darryl Strawberry who could not look anybody in the eye. That was a Darryl Strawberry who nearly wrecked his life and other lives, through drugs and alcohol and other diversions, to avoid facing the world and himself in any sober way.

We never really know how anybody will react to misfortune, but it is reasonable to assume this was not a man who could have faced terrible news with clarity and discipline. Then again, that was not the same Darryl Strawberry who found out today that he must have an operation for colon cancer, perhaps as soon as tomorrow. This Darryl Strawberry is not only physically straight but also mentally and spiritually straight.

Twelve years later, in another baseball season, Darryl Strawberry is now a Yankee, a survivor, a 24–home run hitter. At some time, in one of those treatment centers, he accepted that he had come close to going to jail, that perhaps his

second marriage and his life itself would not survive, unless he stayed sober day by day.

Some people in New York, who felt personally let down by Strawberry, as if he had cost them money, would make condescending comments about him. They did not want to know of his renewal, which was real and tangible, up close.

Oh, he was still the same Straw—the vile odor of his furtive cigarette stinking out a tiny corner of the clubhouse, the bulging chaw inside his cheek (tobacco is indeed a potent addiction), the salty talk, the street wisdom. But Darryl was clean now.

"We have different personalities, but I'm as close to him as anybody in the clubhouse," Bernie Williams said today as the Yankees prepared for Game 3 of the Division Series with the Rangers.

Homer Bush, the earnest rookie, recalled joining the Yankees in 1997 on the same day Strawberry returned from a training stint in the minor leagues. "He talked to me, he told me he liked the way I played, he said I was going to have a good career," Bush said. "He gave me advice."

"He's always been a good person," said David Cone, who knows Strawberry from the wild Met days. "He's made his mistakes, we all have, but he's turned it around. He's a team leader. We're all optimistic he has the strength to beat it."

This may not be much consolation, but this horrible thing has happened to a man whose strength will be even more of a blessing than he could have known.

—*GEORGE VECSEY*

Out of the Blue

SAN DIEGO, Oct. 21—Brian Cashman was still an assistant general manager with the Yankees when an official from the Oakland Athletics raised the possibility of trading Scott Brosius in the fall of 1997.

"I don't think so," Cashman told Billy Beane, then assistant general manager for Oakland. "But let me check with my people." Cashman was negotiating, of course. But he had communicated his own instincts: No way. He knew Brosius was coming off a bad year, and he knew Brosius would be in line to make a decent salary.

But Cashman and Bob Watson, then the Yankee general manager, checked with their scouts, and were assured that Brosius was worth having—and the rest is history.

Brosius hammered two home runs in Game 3 of the World Series and singled home the third run of Game 4 to help the Yankees wrap up their 24th title. The performance helped Brosius nail down the Series' most valuable player award; he finished with 8 hits in 17 times up (.471), including 2 homers and 6 runs batted in. For the 13-game post-season, Brosius batted .383 with 6 homers and 15 r.b.i.

Holding his m.v.p. trophy in a joyous clubhouse, Brosius said: "I don't know what to do with this thing. It's bigger and heavier than anything I've ever gotten."

Brosius batted .300 and drove in 98 runs during the regular season. In the estimation of his teammate Derek Jeter, he was the team's m.v.p.—a pleasant surprise to club executives, who had hoped only that Brosius would play solid defense and contribute a few hits.

"We didn't know exactly what Scott Brosius was all about," said Joe Torre. "You pick up a press guide and you see numbers, and last year he wasn't that good."

An understatement: Brosius was terrible for Oakland in 1997, a year in which "everything that could go bad did," he recalled.

"Everything from just at times swinging the bat horribly to other times swinging the bat pretty good and being unlucky, and just not feeling real healthy, either," Brosius said. "It was just one of those things that kind of snowballed, and I was never able to come out of it."

Brosius batted .203 with 11 home runs and 41 r.b.i. in 1997, with other A's feeling as if his quiet intensity hampered him as his slump deepened. He had batted .304 in 1996, hitting 22 home runs, but given his age of 31, it was easy to speculate he was in decline.

When Beane called Cashman, Cashman had his doubts. But the Yankees needed a third baseman, having determined to allow the aging Wade Boggs to depart as a free agent and to exile Charlie Hayes. Cashman called Ron Brand, the Yankees' West Coast scout.

"This guy can play," Brand told Cashman, noting Brosius' strong defense and the fact that he always played hard and was well liked by teammates. Even if Brosius doesn't hit enough to be the everyday third baseman, Brand said then, he could be an exceptional utilityman.

Today, Brand said: "I heard some guys talk about how he was complaining, but I never saw that in the way he played. I never saw him complaining in the paper. He was always very gracious. He's a model citizen."

By the end of spring training, Brosius had won the third-base job and Torre was talking about how Brosius was the best he had ever seen at charging in and barehanding grounders and throwing to first.

Mike Lowell is waiting for his chance, coming off an exceptional season with Class AAA Columbus, but re-signing Brosius appears to be a priority.

"Ultimately, we'd like to keep him," Cashman said.
—*BUSTER OLNEY*

Nine Years in the Making

ARLINGTON, Tex., Oct. 2—Gordy Thompson, the baseball coach at Granite Hills High School in East San Diego, would open the batting cage during sixth period and Shane Spencer would be there daily, pulling balls into the left side of the cage.

Tim Schmidt, a Yankee scout, first noticed the 18-year-old Spencer's speed, unusual given his thick calves and thighs. He saw a short, compact swing. He did not know if Spencer would hit for power, or become a good outfielder. But he was sure that Spencer loved to play baseball.

Schmidt offered Spencer a small bonus as the 28th-round pick in the 1990 draft and Spencer passed up a college scholarship so he could pursue a dream that 28th-round picks almost never realize. Spencer's passion for the game buoyed him through a nine-season journey to the majors that has brought him here, to sudden and extraordinary fame.

"I am not surprised," said Spencer, 26, who hit 10 home runs in 67 at-bats in the regular season, including three grand slams in 10 days, and homered twice against Texas in the Division Series. "I guess I'm surprised it's all happening at once."

First-round draft picks are pushed to the big leagues; 28th-round draft picks must push themselves. They must produce big numbers and earn attention. Spencer did not do that in his first five seasons. He hit three homers in his first 618 at-bats; in 1994 he batted .290 with 8 homers. Good, but not good enough to push a 28th-round pick to the majors.

Before the 1995 season, Gene Michael, the Yankees' general manager at the time, met with Spencer. "I told him, 'You've got to start putting up numbers,' " Michael recalled. He told Spencer that he would return to Class A for his sixth straight season.

Spencer batted .300 with 16 home runs and 88 runs batted in. A dead-pull hitter for most of his life, he began driving the ball to all fields. He jumped to Class AA the next year and hit 29 home runs, and in 1997 he slugged 30 home runs for Class AAA Columbus. The Yankees did not call him up in September, which disappointed him. "But he just said he needed to work harder," said Althea Olejniczak, his mother. "That's always been his answer: work harder."

It paid off, as Spencer gradually pushed his way into the sights of Yankee officials. They wanted more numbers, he gave them more numbers. They wanted him to improve his defense, he developed into an adequate outfielder. They wanted him to gather experience, and Spencer went to Hawaii, Australia, Venezuela and Arizona to play winter ball. He played well in spring training.

He began the season in Columbus, his ninth year in the minors. But when Chili Davis injured his ankle, Joe Torre asked for the best right-handed hitter in the organization and he got Spencer, who wound up being recalled and sent down three times.

Olejniczak, who had seen her son chase his dream for years, watched his home run in Game 2 against the Rangers at her mother's home in Shirley, Ark., and leapt to her feet screaming, "I can't believe it!" In a bar in Arizona, Schmidt, the scout, yelled and thrust a fist in the air, drawing odd stares.

As Spencer strolled to the plate for that at-bat, Thompson sat in his den in Santee, Calif., remembering how hard he worked, feeling good about the young man he had come to like and respect. When Spencer's ball disappeared over the wall at Yankee Stadium, his high school baseball coach began to cry.

—*BUSTER OLNEY*

A Quiet Rage

NEW YORK, March 29—Bernie Williams usually faces his locker as he plays his guitar in the Yankees' clubhouse, staring forward, everything and everyone left behind him. When approached, he will always turn, unfailingly polite with strangers, warm with teammates, peering gently through wire-framed glasses that could be crumpled with one hand. Outsiders walk away, and Williams turns back and faces his locker. He looks inward again.

A friend said recently that Williams, who can be a free agent after the season, knows pressure will mount on him to justify his desire for an eight-figure salary. Hidden behind the soft demeanor, the friend said, is a furious, introspective competitor who is treating these circumstances as a challenge to his ability. Bernie Williams, the raging bull.

Williams is quiet after his friend's analysis is repeated to him.

Five seconds of silence.

Ten seconds.

"That's pretty accurate right there," Williams says finally.

"I try to be nice, and that could be misunderstood sometimes. I know early in my career, they misunderstood niceness for weakness."

Teammates understand. Watch the way he takes his at-bats, David Cone said, the way he maintains his intensity.

"He never gives away any at-bats," Cone said.

Joe Girardi says that early in the season, Williams will be nearly silent on the bench. In August and September, Williams starts talking, imploring his teammates with a phrase here or there.

"And when he says something, it's sincere," Joe Torre said. "He doesn't make noise just for the sake of making noise."

Williams will play and then retreat to his guitar, play and retreat. He likes his time alone. As a teenager growing up in a relatively rural area of Puerto Rico, he liked to go to a balcony to play folk songs. Williams did not lack for friends then or now; he is extremely well liked. He just likes his time alone, to think, not to think.

"He has got an ability to block anything out," Cone said. "He may be one of the best in terms of concentration, almost a trancelike state when he's in a good groove. Almost hypnotic."

Williams will turn inward, play his guitar, play his game.

—*BUSTER OLNEY*

Williams filed for free agency on Oct. 26.

The Perfect Fit

NEW YORK, Oct. 23—Joe Torre was eating a late dinner with his wife, Ali, on a brisk night in San Diego during the World Series when a question he had occasionally pondered sneaked up on him again. Torre said the words softly across the table: Why me?

Torre was trying to understand why he had been chosen to manage the Yankees three years ago, when it looked as if his managerial career had died forever. He wanted to figure out why he had flourished under George Steinbrenner, coolly chaperoning the Yankees to greatness. What had he done to deserve this opportunity? Why me?

After the Yankees beat the Padres for their second World Series championship in three seasons, every player hugged Torre and thanked him, one by one. Torre was startled. That was supposed to be his line. Why were the players thanking him? Why me?

"Everyone seems to think that I've paid my dues and I have it coming, but I don't see it that way," he said. "I've been really lucky. I wonder why it's happened to me. People who know me don't give it a second thought. I'll rely on their opinions, but knowing that this is all the product of hard work keeps me working hard."

He is the calm leader, the 58-year-old New Yorker who returned home in 1996 against the advice of his brother, Frank, to find his own version of baseball nirvana in the South Bronx. Torre presided, simply and maturely, over a team that won an astounding 125 games. Sometimes it looks easy. But that is only because Torre, his rugged face usually as expressionless as a mannequin's, makes it look that way.

"He's perfect for this city because he makes everything seem like it's not that big of a deal," General Manager Brian Cashman said. "No matter how tough the situation is, he makes it seem like it's not that tough."

There was always something comforting about the way Torre carried himself this season, from the first day of spring training when he called the Yankees "a special team" to the final night of the World Series when he called them "the best team in my lifetime." His players fed off his tranquil disposition. If Joe looked relaxed, then everything must be copacetic, they figured. Usually, it was.

"If you don't like playing for Joe Torre, you better get yourself checked out," said Don Zimmer, the bench coach. "That's the best way I can put it."

Torre could have had a delicate time keeping the Yankees focused after they sprinted out to a 15-game lead by July, but they played with passion every day. The Yankees did it to chase history, but they also did it because of Torre.

"He's the epitome of what a manager should be," Chili Davis said. "It's not about making moves, or running out there and being noticed, or saying I did this or did that. He took 25 players and, whatever he said to us, he made us all want to go out and bust our butts for him."

Torre said: "I show them honesty and I trust them, and I just ask the same in return. It's not always going to be wonderful, but, this sounds pretty corny, it's togetherness. If we win, we win. If we lose, we lose."

Why me? The question still hounded Torre after Game 4.

"Maybe the good Lord didn't think I could appreciate all of it before now," he said. "I know one thing. After doing this the first time, you really want to do it again. This was even sweeter the second time. This was great."

—*JACK CURRY*

Even the laid-back Torre (opposite, pitching batting practice) got a little emotional (above) after the Yankees' victory over Cleveland in the A.L.C.S.

Appendix

G	DATE	OPP		SCORE	RECORD	W	L	S
1	4/1	@ANA	L	1–4	0–1	Finley	Pettitte	Percival
2	4/2	@ANA	L	2–10	0–2	Hill	Wells	
3	4/4	@OAK	L	3–7	0–3	Haynes	Cone	
4	4/5	@OAK	W	9–7 (10)	1–3	Nelson	Mohler	
5	4/6	@SEA	L	0–8	1–4	Moyer	Pettitte	
6	4/7	@SEA	W	13–7	2–4	Wells	Bullinger	
7	4/8	@SEA	W	4–3	3–4	Lloyd	Ayala	Stanton
8	4/10	OAK	W	17–13	4–4	Buddie	Dougherty	
9	4/11	OAK	W	3–1	5–4	Pettitte	Candiotti	Stanton
10	4/12	OAK	W	7–5	6–4	Buddie	Mathews	Stanton
11	4/15	ANA	W	6–3	7–4	Wells	Hill	Nelson
12	4/17	@DET	W	11–2	8–4	Pettitte	Thompson	
13	4/18	@DET	W	8–3	9–4	Cone	Keagle	
14	4/19	@DET	L	1–2	9–5	Moehler	Holmes	Jones
15	4/20	@TOR	W	3–2 (11)	10–5	Banks	Risley	Stanton
16	4/21	@TOR	W	5–3 (10)	11–5	Stanton	Plesac	
17	4/22	@TOR	W	9–1	12–5	Pettitte	Clemens	
18	4/24	DET	W	8–4	13–5	Cone	Keagle	
19	4/25	DET	W	5–4	14–5	Wells	Runyan	Rivera
20	4/27	TOR	W	1–0	15–5	Pettitte	Clemens	Rivera
21	4/28	TOR	L	2–5	15–6	Williams	Mendoza	Myers
22	4/29	SEA	W	8–5	16–6	Cone	Fassero	Rivera
23	4/30	SEA	W	9–8 (10)	17–6	Rivera	Ayala	
24	5/1	@KAN	W	2–1	18–6	Irabu	Rapp	Rivera
25	5/2	@KAN	W	12–6	19–6	Pettitte	Haney	
26	5/3	@KAN	W	10–1	20–6	Mendoza	Belcher	
27	5/5	@TEX	W	7–2	21–6	Cone	Burkett	
28	5/6	@TEX	W	15–13	22–6	Stanton	Patterson	Rivera
29	5/8	@MIN	W	5–1	23–6	Irabu	Radke	Nelson
30	5/9	@MIN	L	1–8	23–7	Morgan	Pettitte	
31	5/10	@MIN	W	7–0	24–7	Mendoza	Milton	
32	5/12	KAN	W	3–2	25–7	Wells	Rusch	Rivera
33	5/13	TEX	W	8–6	26–7	Cone	Helling	Rivera
34	5/14	TEX	L	5–7 (13)	26–8	Patterson	Banks	Wetteland
35	5/15	MIN	L	6–7	26–9	Milton	Pettitte	Aguilera
36	5/16	MIN	W	5–2	27–9	Mendoza	Tewksbury	Rivera
37	5/17	MIN	W	4–0	28–9	Wells	Hawkins	
38	5/19	BAL	W	9–5	29–9	Stanton	Charlton	
39	5/20	BAL	W	9–6	30–9	Irabu	Key	
40	5/21	BAL	W	3–1	31–9	Pettitte	Erickson	Rivera
41	5/22	@BOS	L	4–5	31–10	Wakefield	Nelson	Gordon
42	5/23	@BOS	W	12–3	32–10	Wells	Lowe	
43	5/24	@BOS	W	14–4	33–10	Cone	Saberhagen	
44	5/25	@CHA	W	12–0	34–10	Irabu	Navarro	
45	5/26	@CHA	W	7–5	35–10	Nelson	Foulke	Rivera
46	5/27	@CHA	L	9–12	35–11	Simas	Nelson	Karchner
47	5/28	BOS	W	8–3	36–11	Wells	Wakefield	Stanton
48	5/29	BOS	W	6–2	37–11	Cone	Lowe	
49	5/30	BOS	L	2–3	37–12	Saberhagen	Irabu	Gordon
50	5/31	BOS	L	7–13	37–13	Martinez	Pettitte	
51	6/1	CHA	W	5–4 (10)	38–13	Nelson	Karchner	
52	6/2	CHA	W	6–3	39–13	Wells	Sirotka	Rivera
53	6/3	TAM	W	7–1	40–13	Hernández	Saunders	
54	6/4	TAM	W	6–1	41–13	Irabu	Springer	
55	6/5	FLA	W	5–1	42–13	Pettitte	Fontenot	
56	6/6	FLA	W	4–2	43–13	Mendoza	Sanchez	Rivera
57	6/7	FLA	W	4–1	44–13	Cone	Dempster	
58	6/9	@MON	W	11–1	45–13	Hernández	Perez	
59	6/10	@MON	W	6–2	46–13	Irabu	Hermanson	
60	6/11	@MON	L	5–7	46–14	Valdes	Nelson	Urbina
61	6/14	CLE	W	4–2	47–14	Cone	Wright	Rivera
62	6/15	@BAL	L	4–7	47–15	Erickson	Wells	Orosco
63	6/16	@BAL	L	0–2	47–16	Ponson	Irabu	Rhodes
64	6/17	@BAL	W	5–3	48–16	Pettitte	Mussina	Rivera
65	6/18	@CLE	W	5–2	49–16	Nelson	Assenmacher	Rivera
66	6/19	@CLE	L	4–7	49–17	Wright	Cone	Jackson
67	6/20	@CLE	W	5–3	50–17	Wells	Burba	Rivera
68	6/21	@CLE	L	0–11	50–18	Colon	Irabu	
69	6/22	ATL	W	6–4	51–18	Nelson	Martinez	Rivera
70	6/23	ATL	L	2–7	51–19	Glavine	Hernández	
71	6/24	ATL	W	10–6	52–19	Cone	Millwood	Rivera
72	6/25	ATL	W	6–0	53–19	Wells	Neagle	
73	6/26	@NYM	W	8–4	54–19	Mendoza	Leiter	Rivera
74	6/27	@NYM	W	7–2	55–19	Pettitte	Jones	
75	6/28	@NYM	L	1–2	55–20	Cook	Mendoza	
76	6/30	PHI	W	9–2	56–20	Cone	Loewer	
77	7/1	PHI	W	5–2	57–20	Wells	Beech	Rivera
78	7/2	PHI	W	9–8 (11)	58–20	Buddie	Spradlin	
79	7/3	BAL	W	3–2	59–20	Pettitte	Orosco	
80	7/4	BAL	W	4–3	60–20	Hernández	Drabek	Rivera
81	7/5	BAL	W	1–0	61–20	Cone	Erickson	Rivera
82	7/9	@TAM	W	2–0	62–20	Pettitte	Rekar	Rivera
83	7/10	@TAM	W	8–4	63–20	Irabu	Alvarez	Mendoza
84	7/11	@TAM	W	2–0	64–20	Cone	Arrojo	Rivera
85	7/12	@TAM	W	9–2	65–20	Stanton	Hernandez	
86	7/13	@CLE	L	1–4	65–21	Wright	Hernández	Jackson
87	7/14	@CLE	W	7–1	66–21	Pettitte	Burba	
88	7/15	@DET	W	11–0	67–21	Irabu	Greisinger	
89	7/16	@DET	L	1–3	67–22	Moehler	Cone	Jones
90	7/17	@TOR	L	6–9	67–23	Clemens	Holmes	Myers
91	7/18	@TOR	W	10–3	68–23	Hernández	Guzman	
92	7/19	@TOR	L	3–9	68–24	Williams	Pettitte	
93	7/20	DET	L	3–4 (17)	68–25	Sager	Holmes	
94	7/20	DET	W	4–3	69–25	Irabu	Florie	Rivera
95	7/21	DET	W	5–1	70–25	Cone	Moehler	
96	7/22	DET	W	13–2	71–25	Hernández	Powell	Holmes
97	7/24	CHA	W	5–4	72–25	Pettitte	Ward	Rivera
98	7/25	CHA	L	2–6	72–26	Sirotka	Irabu	Simas
99	7/26	CHA	W	6–3	73–26	Wells	Navarro	Rivera
100	7/28	@ANA	W	9–3	74–26	Cone	Dickson	
101	7/29	@ANA	L	5–10	74–27	Sparks	Hernández	
102	7/30	@ANA	W	3–0 (10)	75–27	Mendoza	Delucia	Rivera
103	7/31	@SEA	W	5–3	76–27	Irabu	Fassero	Rivera
104	8/1	@SEA	W	5–2	77–27	Wells	Moyer	
105	8/2	@SEA	L	3–6	77–28	Wells	Cone	Timlin
106	8/3	@OAK	W	14–1	78–28	Hernández	Oquist	
107	8/4	@OAK	W	10–4	79–28	Mendoza	Witasick	Stanton
108	8/4	@OAK	W	10–5	80–28	Lloyd	Taylor	
109	8/5	@OAK	L	1–3	80–29	Candiotti	Irabu	
110	8/7	KAN	W	8–2	81–29	Cone	Rapp	
111	8/7	KAN	W	14–2	82–29	Wells	Haney	
112	8/8	KAN	W	14–1	83–29	Hernández	Rusch	
113	8/9	KAN	W	5–4	84–29	Mendoza	Service	Rivera
114	8/10	MIN	W	7–3	85–29	Irabu	Rodriguez	
115	8/11	MIN	W	7–0	86–29	Wells	Milton	
116	8/12	MIN	W	11–2	87–29	Cone	Hawkins	
117	8/13	TEX	W	2–0	88–29	Hernández	Helling	Rivera
118	8/14	TEX	W	6–4	89–29	Pettitte	Sele	Rivera

G	DATE	OPP		SCORE	RECORD	W	L	S
119	8/15	TEX	L	5–16	89–30	Stottlemyre	Irabu	
120	8/16	TEX	W	6–5	90–30	Rivera	Hernandez	
121	8/17	@KAN	W	7–1	91–30	Cone	Rosado	
122	8/18	@KAN	W	3–2 (13)	92–30	Borowski	Whisenant	
123	8/19	@MIN	L	3–5	92–31	Serafini	Pettitte	Aguilera
124	8/20	@MIN	L	4–9	92–32	Rodriguez	Buddie	
125	8/21	@TEX	W	5–0	93–32	Wells	Loaiza	
126	8/22	@TEX	W	12–9	94–32	Bradley	Hernandez	Rivera
127	8/23	@TEX	L	10–12	94–33	Helling	Hernández	Wetteland
128	8/24	ANA	L	3–7	94–34	McDowell	Pettitte	
129	8/25	ANA	L	6–7	94–35	Watson	Stanton	Percival
130	8/26	ANA	L	4–6	94–36	Juden	Bradley	Percival
131	8/26	ANA	W	7–6	95–36	Rivera	Fetters	
132	8/27	ANA	W	6–5 (11)	96–36	Tessmer	Fetters	
133	8/28	SEA	W	10–3	97–36	Hernández	Spoljaric	
134	8/29	SEA	W	11–6	98–36	Pettitte	Cloude	
135	8/30	SEA	L	3–13	98–37	Swift	Irabu	
136	9/1	OAK	W	7–0	99–37	Wells	Candiotti	
137	9/2	OAK	L	0–2	99–38	Heredia	Cone	Taylor
138	9/4	@CHA	W	11–6	100–38	Lloyd	Bradford	
139	9/5	@CHA	L	5–9	100–39	Abbott	Pettitte	
140	9/6	@CHA	L	5–6	100–40	Baldwin	Irabu	Howry
141	9/7	@BOS	L	3–4	100–41	Swindell	Wells	Gordon
142	9/8	@BOS	W	3–2	101–41	Cone	Martinez	Rivera
143	9/9	@BOS	W	7–5	102–41	Mendoza	Wakefield	Rivera
144	9/10	TOR	W	8–5	103–41	Pettitte	Hentgen	Holmes
145	9/11	TOR	L	4–5	103–42	Almanzar	Irabu	Person
146	9/12	TOR	L	3–5	103–43	Carpenter	Wells	Person
147	9/13	TOR	L	3–5	103–44	Escobar	Cone	Person
148	9/14	BOS	W	3–0	104–44	Hernández	Martinez	
149	9/15	BOS	L	4–9	104–45	Wakefield	Jerzembeck	

G	DATE	OPP		SCORE	RECORD	W	L	S
150	9/16	@TAM	L	0–7	104–46	Saunders	Pettitte	
151	9/17	@TAM	W	4–0	105–46	Irabu	Santana	
152	9/18	@BAL	W	15–5	106–46	Wells	Guzman	
153	9/19	@BAL	L	3–5	106–47	Ponson	Cone	Mills
154	9/20	@BAL	W	5–4	107–47	Hernández	Johns	Rivera
155	9/21	CLE	L	1–4	107–48	Nagy	Pettitte	Shuey
156	9/22	CLE	W	10–4	108–48	Mendoza	Burba	
157	9/22	CLE	W	5–1	109–48	Irabu	Ogea	
158	9/23	CLE	W	8–4	110–48	Bradley	Jacome	
159	9/24	TAM	W	5–2	111–48	Buddie	Alvarez	Nelson
160	9/25	TAM	W	6–1	112–48	Hernández	Eiland	
161	9/26	TAM	W	3–1	113–48	Cone	Wade	
162	9/27	TAM	W	8–3	114–48	Bruske	White	

DIVISION SERIES

G	DATE	OPP		SCORE	RECORD	W	L	S
163	9/29	TEX	W	2–0	115–48	Wells	Stottlemyre	Rivera
164	9/30	TEX	W	3–1	116–48	Pettitte	Helling	Rivera
165	10/2	@TEX	W	4–0	117–48	Cone	Sele	

AMERICAN LEAGUE CHAMPIONSHIP SERIES

G	DATE	OPP		SCORE	RECORD	W	L	S
166	10/6	CLE	W	7–2	118–48	Wells	Wright	
167	10/7	CLE	L	1–4 (12)	118–49	Burba	Nelson	Jackson
168	10/9	@CLE	L	1–6	118–50	Colon	Pettitte	
169	10/10	@CLE	W	4–0	119–50	Hernández	Gooden	
170	10/11	@CLE	W	5–3	120–50	Wells	Ogea	Rivera
171	10/13	CLE	W	9–5	121–50	Cone	Nagy	

WORLD SERIES

G	DATE	OPP		SCORE	RECORD	W	L	S
172	10/17	SD	W	9–6	122–50	Wells	Wall	Rivera
173	10/18	SD	W	9–3	123–50	Hernández	Ashby	
174	10/20	@SD	W	5–4	124–50	Mendoza	Hoffman	Rivera
175	10/21	@SD	W	3–0	125–50	Pettitte	Brown	Rivera

REGULAR SEASON STATISTICS

BATTING	BA	G	AB	R	H	TB	2B	3B	HR	RBI	SB	BB	SO
Bush, Homer	.380	45	71	17	27	33	3	0	1	5	6	5	19
Spencer, Shane	.373	27	67	18	25	61	6	0	10	27	0	5	12
Williams, Bernie	.339	128	499	101	169	287	30	5	26	97	15	74	81
Jeter, Derek	.324	149	626	127	203	307	25	8	19	84	30	57	119
O'Neill, Paul	.317	152	602	95	191	307	40	2	24	116	15	57	103
Brosius, Scott	.300	152	530	86	159	250	34	0	19	98	11	52	97
Davis, Chili	.291	35	103	11	30	46	7	0	3	9	0	14	18
Raines, Tim	.290	109	321	53	93	123	13	1	5	47	8	55	49
Martinez, Tino	.281	142	531	92	149	268	33	1	28	123	2	61	83
Girardi, Joe	.276	78	254	31	70	98	11	4	3	31	2	14	38
Posada, Jorge	.268	111	358	56	96	170	23	0	17	63	0	47	92
Knoblauch, Chuck	.265	150	603	117	160	244	25	4	17	64	31	76	70
Strawberry, Darryl	.247	101	295	44	73	160	11	2	24	57	8	46	90
Curtis, Chad	.243	151	456	79	111	164	21	1	10	56	21	75	80
Ledee, Ricky	.241	42	79	13	19	31	5	2	1	12	3	7	29
Sojo, Luis	.231	54	147	16	34	39	3	1	0	14	1	4	15

PITCHING	ERA	W	L	G	GS	CG	SV	INN	H	R	ER	BB	SO
Lloyd, Graeme	1.67	3	0	50	0	0	0	37⅔	26	10	7	6	20
Rivera, Mariano	1.91	3	0	54	0	0	36	61⅓	48	13	13	17	36
Hernández, Orlando	3.13	12	4	21	21	3	0	141	113	53	49	52	131
Mendoza, Ramiro	3.25	10	2	41	14	1	1	130⅓	131	50	47	30	56
Holmes, Darren	3.33	0	3	34	0	0	2	51½	53	19	19	14	31
Wells, David	3.49	18	4	30	30	8	0	214⅓	195	86	83	29	163
Cone, David	3.55	20	7	31	31	3	0	207⅔	186	89	82	59	209
Nelson, Jeff	3.79	5	3	45	0	0	3	40½	44	18	17	22	35
Irabu, Hideki	4.06	13	9	29	28	2	0	173	148	79	78	76	126
Pettitte, Andy	4.24	16	11	33	32	5	0	216⅓	226	110	102	87	146
Stanton, Mike	5.47	4	1	67	0	0	6	79	71	51	48	26	69
Buddie, Mike	5.62	4	1	24	2	0	0	41⅔	46	29	26	13	20

MAJOR LEAGUE RECORDS

- **Most victories (regular season and playoffs)**—125
- **Most World Series titles**—24
- **Most consecutive games holding a lead**—48
- **Most victories before the All-Star break**—61
- **Earliest date to record 100 victories**—Sept. 4
- **Most home runs without a single player hitting 30**—207
- **Highest winning percentage in a 162-game season**—.704
- **Most consecutive winning series**—24 (tied with 1912 Red Sox and '70 Reds)
- **Most players in double figures in both home runs and stolen bases**—6 (tied with '91 Reds): Brosius—19/11; Curtis—10/21; Jeter—19/30; Knoblauch—17/30; O'Neill—24/15; and Williams—26/15
- **Most players with 15 or more home runs**—8 (tied with '91 Rangers): Strawberry, Martinez, O'Neill, Williams, Knoblauch, Jeter, Posada and Brosius
- **Most consecutive months with winning percentage of .700 or more**—4 (record since turn of century)
- **Fewest games to reach 90 victories**—120 (tied with '44 Cardinals)

AMERICAN LEAGUE RECORDS

- **Most victories in a single season**—114
- **Fewest games to reach 100 victories**—138

TEAM RECORDS

- **Widest margin of season victory**—22 games over second-place Red Sox
- **Most games over .500**—66 (tied with '27 Yankees [110–44])

DIVISON SERIES COMPOSITE BOX SCORE

NEW YORK YANKEES

BATTING	AB	R	H	HR	RBI	Avg
Curtis	3	1	2	0	0	.667
Spencer	6	3	3	2	4	.500
Girardi	7	0	3	0	0	.429
Brosius	10	1	4	1	3	.400
O'Neill	11	1	4	1	1	.364
Martinez	11	1	3	0	0	.273
Raines	4	1	1	0	0	.250
Davis	6	0	1	0	0	.167
Jeter	9	0	1	0	0	.111
Knoblauch	11	0	1	0	0	.091
Posada	2	1	0	0	0	.000
Williams	11	0	0	0	0	.000
Totals	91	9	23	4	8	.253

PITCHING	G	IP	H	BB	SO	ERA
Cone	1	5⅔	2	1	6	0.00
Lloyd	1	⅓	0	0	0	0.00
Nelson	2	2⅔	2	1	2	0.00
Rivera	3	3⅓	1	1	2	0.00
Wells	1	8	5	1	9	0.00
Pettitte	1	7	3	0	8	1.29
Totals	3	27	13	4	27	0.33

TEXAS RANGERS

BATTING	AB	R	H	HR	RBI	Avg
Zeile	9	0	3	0	0	.333
Goodwin	4	0	1	0	0	.250
Clayton	9	0	2	0	0	.222
Simms	5	0	1	0	0	.200
Kelly	7	0	1	0	0	.143
McLemore	10	0	1	0	0	.100
Rodriguez	10	0	1	0	1	.100
Clark	11	0	1	0	0	.091
Greer	11	0	1	0	0	.091
Gonzalez	12	1	1	0	0	.083
Alicea	1	0	0	0	0	.000
Stevens	3	0	0	0	0	.000
Totals	92	1	13	0	1	.141

PITCHING	G	IP	H	BB	SO	ERA
Crabtree	2	4	1	0	2	0.00
Wetteland	1	1	0	1	1	0.00
Stottlemyre	1	8	6	4	8	2.25
Helling	1	6	8	1	9	4.50
Sele	1	6	8	1	4	6.00
Totals	3	25	23	7	24	3.24

ALCS COMPOSITE BOX SCORES

NEW YORK YANKEES

BATTING	AB	R	H	HR	RBI	Avg
Williams	21	4	8	0	5	.381
Brosius	20	2	6	1	6	.300
Davis	14	2	4	1	5	.286
O'Neill	25	6	7	1	3	.280
Girardi	8	2	2	0	0	.250
Jeter	25	3	5	0	2	.200
Knoblauch	25	4	5	0	0	.200
Posada	11	1	2	1	2	.182
Martinez	19	1	2	0	1	.105
Raines	10	0	1	0	1	.100
Spencer	10	1	1	0	0	.100
Curtis	4	0	0	0	0	.000
Ledee	5	0	0	0	0	.000
Bush	0	0	0	0	0	—
Totals	197	19	43	4	25	.218

PITCHING	G	IP	H	BB	SO	ERA
Hernández	1	7	3	2	6	0.00
Rivera	4	5⅔	0	1	5	0.00
Mendoza	2	4⅓	4	0	1	0.00
Stanton	3	3⅔	2	1	4	0.00
Lloyd	1	⅔	1	0	0	0.00
Wells	2	15⅔	12	2	18	2.87
Cone	2	13	12	6	13	4.15
Pettitte	1	4⅔	8	3	1	11.57
Nelson	3	1⅓	3	1	3	20.26
Totals	6	56	45	16	51	3.21

CLEVELAND INDIANS

BATTING	AB	R	H	HR	RBI	Avg
Vizquel	25	2	11	0	0	.440
M. Ramirez	21	2	7	2	4	.333
Thome	23	4	7	4	8	.304
Whiten	7	2	2	1	1	.286
E. Wilson	14	2	3	0	1	.214
Lofton	27	2	5	1	3	.185
Fryman	23	2	4	0	0	.174
Justice	19	2	3	1	2	.158
Cora	7	1	1	0	0	.143
Giles	12	0	1	0	0	.083
S. Alomar	16	1	1	0	0	.063
3 others	11	0	0	0	0	.000
Totals	205	20	45	9	19	.220

PITCHING	G	IP	H	BB	SO	ERA
Shuey	5	6⅓	4	7	7	0.00
Assenmacher	3	2	0	0	3	0.00
Reed	3	1⅔	0	1	0	0.00
Poole	4	1⅓	0	1	2	0.00
Jackson	1	1	0	0	2	0.00
Colon	1	9	4	4	3	1.00
Burba	3	6	3	5	8	3.00
Nagy	2	9⅔	13	1	6	3.72
Gooden	1	4⅔	3	3	3	5.79
Ogea	2	6⅔	9	5	4	8.10
Wright	2	6⅔	7	8	4	8.10
Totals	6	55	43	35	42	3.60

WORLD SERIES COMPOSITE BOX SCORES

NEW YORK YANKEES

BATTING	AB	R	H	HR	RBI	Avg
Ledee	10	1	6	0	4	.600
Cone	2	0	1	0	0	.500
Brosius	17	3	8	2	6	.471
Martinez	13	4	5	1	4	.385
Knoblauch	16	3	6	1	3	.375
Jeter	17	4	6	0	1	.353
Posada	9	2	3	1	2	.333
Spencer	3	1	1	0	0	.333
Davis	7	3	2	0	2	.286
O'Neill	19	3	4	0	0	.211
Williams	16	2	1	1	3	.063
M. Rivera	1	0	0	0	0	.000
Mendoza	1	0	0	0	0	.000
Pettitte	2	0	0	0	0	.000
Girardi	6	0	0	0	0	.000
Totals	139	26	43	6	25	.309

PITCHING	G	IP	H	BB	SO	ERA
Pettitte	1	7⅓	5	3	4	0.00
M. Rivera	3	4⅓	5	0	4	0.00
Nelson	3	2⅓	2	1	4	0.00
Lloyd	1	⅓	0	0	0	0.00
O. Hernandez	1	7	6	3	7	1.29
Cone	1	6	2	3	4	3.00
Wells	1	7	7	2	4	6.43
Mendoza	1	2	2	0	1	9.00
Stanton	1	⅔	3	0	1	27.00
Totals	4	36	32	12	29	2.75

SAN DIEGO PADRES

BATTING	AB	R	H	HR	RBI	Avg
R. Rivera	5	1	4	0	1	.800
Sweeney	3	0	2	0	1	.667
Gwynn	16	2	8	1	3	.500
Brown	2	0	1	0	0	.500
Hitchcock	2	1	1	0	0	.500
Vander Wal	5	0	2	0	0	.400
Gomez	11	2	4	0	0	.364
Veras	15	3	3	0	1	.200
C. Hernandez	10	0	2	0	0	.200
Caminiti	14	1	2	0	1	.143
Vaughn	15	3	2	2	4	.133
Finley	12	0	1	0	0	.083
Sheets	2	0	0	0	0	.000
G. Myers	4	0	0	0	0	.000
Joyner	8	0	0	0	0	.000
Leyritz	10	0	0	0	0	.000
Totals	134	13	32	3	11	.239

PITCHING	G	IP	H	BB	SO	ERA
Miceli	2	1⅔	2	2	1	0.00
Hamilton	1	1	0	1	1	0.00
Hitchcock	1	6	7	1	7	1.50
Brown	2	14⅓	14	6	13	4.40
Wall	2	2⅔	3	3	1	6.75
Boehringer	2	2	4	2	3	9.00
Hoffman	2	2	2	1	0	9.00
R. Myers	3	1	0	1	2	9.00
Ashby	1	2⅔	10	1	1	13.50
Langston	1	⅔	1	2	0	40.50
Totals	4	34	43	20	29	5.82

Game 1

SAN DIEGO	AB	R	H	RBI	BB	SO	LOB	AVG
Veras 2b	4	1	1	0	1	0	1	.250
Gwynn rf	4	1	3	2	0	0	0	.750
Vaughn lf	4	3	2	3	0	0	2	.500
Caminiti 3b	3	0	0	0	1	2	1	.000
Leyritz dh	4	0	0	0	0	2	2	.000
Joyner 1b	3	0	0	0	1	1	2	.000
Finley cf	4	0	1	0	0	0	3	.250
Hernandez c	3	0	0	0	0	0	1	.000
a-G. Myers ph	1	0	0	0	0	1	0	.000
Gomez ss	3	1	1	0	0	0	0	.333
b-Vander Wal ph	1	0	0	0	0	1	0	.000
Totals	34	6	8	5	3	7	12	

a—struck out for Hernandez in the 9th; b—struck out for Gomez in the 9th.

NY YANKEES	AB	R	H	RBI	BB	SO	LOB	AVG
Knoblauch 2b	4	1	2	3	0	1	2	.500
Jeter ss	4	1	1	0	1	0	0	.250
O'Neill rf	5	0	0	0	0	1	6	.000
Williams cf	4	1	0	0	1	3	3	.000
Davis dh	3	2	1	0	1	0	0	.333
Martinez 1b	3	2	1	4	1	1	0	.333
Brosius 3b	4	0	1	0	0	1	2	.250
Posada c	3	1	1	0	1	1	0	.333
Ledee lf	3	1	2	2	1	0	0	.667
Totals	33	9	9	9	6	8	13	

San Diego	0 0 2	0 3 0	0 1 0	—6 8 1
New York	0 2 0	0 0 0	7 0 x	—9 9 1

E—San Diego: Vaughn (1); New York: Knoblauch (1). **LOB**—San Diego 4, New York 7. **2B**—San Diego: Finley (1); New York: Ledee (1). **HR**—San Diego: Vaughn 2 (2); New York: Knoblauch (1), Martinez (1). **GIDP**—San Diego: Vaughn.

SAN DIEGO	IP	H	R	ER	BB	SO	HR	ERA
Brown	6⅓	6	4	4	3	5	0	5.68
Wall (L, 0–1)	0	2	2	2	0	0	1	0.00
Langston	⅔	1	3	3	2	0	1	40.50
Boehringer	⅓	0	0	0	1	1	0	0.00
R. Myers	⅔	0	0	0	0	2	0	0.00

NY YANKEES	IP	H	R	ER	BB	SO	HR	ERA
Wells (W, 1–0)	7	7	5	5	2	4	3	6.43
Nelson	⅔	1	1	0	1	1	0	0.00
Rivera (S, 1)	1⅓	0	0	0	0	2	0	0.00

Wall pitched to 2 batters in the 7th.
WP—Langston. IBB—Williams (by Langston). HBP—Knoblauch (by Boehringer).

T—3:29. **A**—56,712.

Game 2

SAN DIEGO	AB	R	H	RBI	BB	SO	LOB	AVG
Veras 2b	5	0	1	1	0	3	4	.222
Gwynn rf	4	0	1	0	1	0	1	.500
Vaughn dh	4	0	0	0	1	1	3	.250
Caminiti 3b	5	1	1	0	0	2	2	.125
Joyner 1b	2	0	0	0	1	0	2	.000
a-Leyritz ph-1b	1	0	0	0	0	1	1	.000
Finley cf	4	0	0	0	0	1	1	.125
Vander Wal lf	3	0	2	0	0	1	0	.500
b-R. Rivera ph-lf	1	1	1	1	0	0	0	1.000
G. Myers c	3	0	0	0	0	1	2	.000
c-Hernandez ph-c	1	0	1	0	0	0	0	.250
Gomez ss	3	1	2	0	0	0	1	.500
d-Sweeney ph	1	0	1	1	0	0	0	1.000
Sheets ss	0	0	0	0	0	0	0	.000
Totals	37	3	10	3	3	10	17	

a—struck out for Joyner in the 8th; b—doubled for Vander Wal in the 8th; c—singled for G Myers in the 8th; d—singled for Gomez in the 8th.

Game 2 (cont.)

NY YANKEES	AB	R	H	RBI	BB	SO	LOB	AVG
Knoblauch 2b	3	2	2	0	2	1	1	.571
Jeter ss	5	1	2	1	0	1	5	.333
O'Neill rf	5	1	1	0	0	0	4	.100
Williams cf	4	1	1	2	1	0	1	.125
Davis dh	3	1	1	1	2	2	1	.333
Bush pr-dh	0	0	0	0	0	0	0	.000
Martinez 1b	5	1	3	0	0	0	3	.500
Brosius 3b	5	1	3	1	0	1	5	.444
Posada c	4	1	1	2	1	0	6	.286
Ledee lf	3	0	2	1	1	0	1	.667
Totals	37	9	16	8	7	5	27	

San Diego	0 0 0	0 1 0	0 2 0	—3 10 1
New York	3 3 1	0 2 0	0 0 x	—9 16 0

E—San Diego: Caminiti (1). **LOB**—San Diego 10, New York 11. **2B**—San Diego: Veras (1), Vander Wal (1), Caminiti (1), R. Rivera (1). New York: Ledee (2). **3B**—San Diego: Gomez (1). **HR**—New York: Williams (1), Posada (1). **SB**—New York: Knoblauch (1). **CS**—New York: Ledee (1). **GIDP**—New York: Posada, Brosius, Jeter.

SAN DIEGO	IP	H	R	ER	BB	SO	HR	ERA
Ashby (L, 0–1)	2⅔	10	7	4	1	1	1	13.50
Boehringer	1⅔	4	2	2	1	2	1	9.00
Wall	2⅔	1	0	0	3	1	0	6.75
Miceli	1	1	0	0	2	1	0	0.00

NY YANKEES	IP	H	R	ER	BB	SO	HR	ERA
Hernández (W, 1–0)	7	6	1	1	3	7	0	1.29
Stanton	⅔	3	2	2	0	1	0	27.00
Nelson	1⅓	1	0	0	0	2	0	0.00

T—3:31. **A**—56,692.

Game 3

NY YANKEES	AB	R	H	RBI	BB	SO	LOB	AVG
Knoblauch 2b	4	0	1	0	1	0	0	.455
Jeter ss	4	0	1	0	1	1	4	.308
O'Neill rf	4	1	1	0	1	1	2	.143
Williams cf	4	0	0	0	0	2	5	.083
Martinez 1b	3	1	0	0	1	0	3	.364
Brosius 3b	4	2	3	4	0	0	0	.538
Spencer lf	3	1	1	0	0	2	1	.333
c-Ledee ph-lf	1	0	0	0	0	0	0	.571
Girardi c	2	0	0	0	0	1	1	.000
a-Posada ph-c	2	0	1	0	0	1	1	.333
Cone p	2	0	1	0	0	0	0	.500
b-Davis ph	1	0	0	1	0	0	1	.286
Bush pr	0	0	0	0	0	0	0	.000
Lloyd p	0	0	0	0	0	0	0	.000
Mendoza p	1	0	0	0	0	0	1	.000
M. Rivera p	0	0	0	0	0	0	0	.000
Totals	35	5	9	5	4	8	19	

a—struck out for Girardi in the 7th; b—reached on error for Cone in the 7th; c—grounded to second for Spencer in the 8th.

SAN DIEGO	AB	R	H	RBI	BB	SO	LOB	AVG
Veras 2b	3	2	1	0	1	0	0	.250
Gwynn rf	4	1	2	1	0	0	0	.500
R. Rivera pr-rf	0	0	0	0	0	0	0	1.000
Vaughn lf	3	0	0	1	0	0	2	.182
Caminiti 3b	2	0	0	1	1	2	1	.100
Joyner 1b	3	0	0	0	1	0	1	.000
Finley cf	4	0	0	0	0	1	1	.083
Leyritz c	2	0	0	0	0	1	1	.000
C. Hernandez	2	0	1	0	0	1	0	.333
Vander Wal pr	0	0	0	0	0	0	0	.500
Gomez ss	3	0	1	0	0	1	0	.444
Hoffman p	0	0	0	0	0	0	0	.000
a-Sweeney ph	1	0	1	0	0	0	0	1.000
Hitchcock p	2	1	1	0	0	0	0	.500
Hamilton p	0	0	0	0	0	0	0	.000
R. Myers p	0	0	0	0	0	0	0	.000
Sheets ss	2	0	0	0	0	1	2	.000
Totals	31	4	7	3	3	7	8	

a—singled for C. Hernandez in the 9th.

Game 3 (cont.)

New York	0 0 0	0 0 0	2 3 0	—5 9 1
San Diego	0 0 0	0 0 3	0 1 0	—4 7 1

E—New York: O'Neill (1); San Diego: Caminiti (2). **LOB**—New York 7, San Diego 5. **2B**—New York: Spencer (1); San Diego: Veras (2). **HR**—New York: Brosius 2 (2). **SB**—San Diego: Finley (1). **Sac**—San Diego: Caminiti (fly), Vaughn (fly). **GIDP**—New York: O'Neill.

NY YANKEES	IP	H	R	ER	BB	SO	HR	ERA
Cone	6	2	3	2	3	4	0	3.00
Lloyd	⅓	0	0	0	0	0	0	0.00
Mendoza (W, 1–0)	1	2	1	1	0	1	0	9.00
M. Rivera (S, 2)	1⅔	3	0	0	0	2	0	0.00

SAN DIEGO	IP	H	R	ER	BB	SO	HR	ERA
Hitchcock	6	7	2	1	1	7	1	1.50
Hamilton	1	0	0	0	1	1	0	0.00
R. Myers	0	0	1	1	1	0	0	13.50
Hoffman (L, 0–1)	2	2	2	2	1	0	1	9.00

Hitchcock pitched to 2 batters in the 7th.
R. Myers pitched to 1 batter in the 8th.

T—3:14. **A**—64,667.

Game 4

NY YANKEES	AB	R	H	RBI	BB	SO	LOB	AVG
Knoblauch 2b	5	0	1	0	0	0	1	.375
Jeter ss	4	2	2	0	1	1	1	.353
O'Neill rf	5	1	2	0	0	0	1	.211
Williams cf	4	0	0	1	0	0	1	.063
Martinez 1b	2	0	1	0	2	1	0	.385
Brosius 3b	4	0	1	1	0	2	3	.471
Ledee lf	3	0	2	1	0	1	2	.600
Girardi c	4	0	0	0	0	1	5	.000
Pettitte p	2	0	0	0	0	2	2	.000
Nelson p	0	0	0	0	0	0	0	.000
M. Rivera p	1	0	0	0	0	0	0	.000
Totals	34	3	9	3	3	8	16	

SAN DIEGO	AB	R	H	RBI	BB	SO	LOB	AVG
Veras 2b	3	0	0	0	1	1	1	.200
Gwynn rf	4	0	2	0	0	0	0	.500
Vaughn lf	4	0	0	0	0	1	3	.133
Caminiti 3b	4	0	1	0	0	1	1	.143
Leyritz 1b	3	0	0	0	1	0	3	.000
R. Rivera cf	4	0	3	0	0	0	0	.800
C. Hernandez c	4	0	0	0	0	2	3	.200
Gomez ss	2	0	0	0	1	0	1	.364
b-Sweeney ph	1	0	0	0	0	0	0	.667
Brown p	2	0	1	0	0	0	3	.500
a-Vander Wal ph	1	0	0	0	0	0	0	.400
Miceli p	0	0	0	0	0	0	0	.000
R. Myers p	0	0	0	0	0	0	0	.000
Totals	32	0	7	0	3	5	15	

a—flied to center for Brown in the 8th; b—grounded to third for Gomez in the 9th.

New York	0 0 0	0 1 0	0 2 0	—3 9 0
San Diego	0 0 0	0 0 0	0 0 0	—0 7 0

LOB—New York 9, San Diego 8. **2B**—New York: Ledee (3), O'Neill (1); San Diego: R. Rivera (2). **Sac**—New York, Pettitte (bunt), Ledee (fly). **GIDP**—San Diego: Caminiti, C. Hernandez.

NY YANKEES	IP	H	R	ER	BB	SO	HR	ERA
Pettitte (W, 1–0)	7⅓	5	0	0	3	4	0	0.00
Nelson	⅓	0	0	0	0	1	0	0.00
M Rivera (S, 3)	1⅓	2	0	0	0	0	0	0.00

SAN DIEGO	IP	H	R	ER	BB	SO	HR	ERA
Brown (L, 0–1)	8	8	3	3	3	8	0	4.40
Miceli	⅔	1	0	0	0	0	0	0.00
R. Myers	⅓	0	0	0	0	0	0	9.00

IBB—Martinez 2 (by Brown 2).

T—2:58. **A**—65,427.

Photo Credits

Cover: Chang W. Lee.
Back cover: Chester Higgins Jr.

Front Matter
Half-title page, Barton Silverman; Title page, G. Paul Burnett.

Introduction
8, Pat Burns; 9, Ernie Sisto; 10, D. Gorton, 11, Larry C. Morris.

The Regular Season
12-13, Barton Silverman; 14, Barton Silverman; 15, Barton Silverman; 16, Chang W. Lee; 17 left, G. Paul Burnett; 17 right, Barton Silverman; 18, top, Barton Silverman; middle, Michelle V. Agins; 19, Barton Silverman; 20, Barton Silverman; 21 (both), Barton Silverman; 22, G. Paul Burnett; 23, Barton Silverman; 24 (both), Chang W. Lee; 25, Chang W. Lee; 26, Barton Silverman; 27 top, Barton Silverman; bottom, Chang W. Lee; 28 top, Barton Silverman; bottom, Chang W. Lee; 29, Michelle V. Agins; 30, Barton Silverman; 31 (both), Barton Silverman; 32 top, Michelle V. Agins; bottom, Barton Silverman; 33, G. Paul Burnett; 34, Barton Silverman; 35 (both), Barton Silverman.

The Playoffs
36-37, G. Paul Burnett; 38, Barton Silverman; 39, Barton Silverman; 40, Chang W. Lee; 41, Barton Silverman; 42, Chang W. Lee; 43, Ozier Muhammad; 44 top, G. Paul Burnett; middle, Barton Silverman; 45 (both), G. Paul Burnett; 47, Ozier Muhammad; 48, Barton Silverman; 49, Barton Silverman; 50, Ozier Muhammad; 50-51, AP; 51, Eileen Blass/USA Today; 52, Chang W. Lee; 53, Chang W. Lee; 54, Barton Silverman; 55, Barton Silverman; 56 (both), Barton Silverman; 57, G. Paul Burnett; 58, Barton Silverman; 59, Barton Silverman; 60, Barton Silverman; 61, Barton Silverman; 62, Barton Silverman; 64, Barton Silverman; 65, Barton Silverman; 67, Ozier Muhammad; 68, G. Paul Burnett; 69 top, G. Paul Burnett; bottom, Barton Silverman.

The World Series
70-71, Barton Silverman; 72, Barton Silverman; 73, Ozier Muhammad; 74, Barton Silverman; 75, Chang W. Lee; 76, Ozier Muhammad; 78, Barton Silverman; 79, Chang W. Lee; 80, Chang W. Lee; 81, Ozier Muhammad; 82, G. Paul Burnett; 83, G. Paul Burnett; 84, G. Paul Burnett; 86 top, Barton Silverman; bottom, G. Paul Burnett; 87, Chang W. Lee; 88 left, G. Paul Burnett; top right, G. Paul Burnett; bottom right, AFP/Timothy A. Clary; 89 left, Chang W. Lee; right, AP/Eric Draper; 90 top, Barton Silverman; bottom, Chang W. Lee; 91, AP/Pat Sullivan; 92 left, Ozier Muhammad; right, Chester Higgins Jr.; 93 top left, Suzanne DeChillo; top right, Marilynn K. Yee; bottom left, Ozier Muhammad; bottom right, Marilynn K. Yee.

Yankee People
94-95, Barton Silverman; 96, G. Paul Burnett; 97, Chang W. Lee; 98, G. Paul Burnett; 99, G. Paul Burnett; 100, G. Paul Burnett; 101, Barton Silverman; 102, Chang W. Lee; 104, G. Paul Burnett; 105, Chang W. Lee; 106-107, Barton Silverman.